Yoruba Grammar and Cultural Guide

by Abraham Ajibade Adeleke

Note for Librarians: A cataloguing record for this book is available from
Library and Archives Canada at www.collectionscanada.ca/amicus/index-e.html
ISBN 1-4120-8531-4

Printed in Victoria, BC, Canada. Printed on paper with minimum 30% recycled fibre.
Trafford's print shop runs on "green energy" from solar, wind and other environmentally-friendly power sources.

Offices in Canada, USA, Ireland and UK

Book sales for North America and international:
Trafford Publishing, 6E–2333 Government St.,
Victoria, BC V8T 4P4 CANADA
phone 250 383 6864 (toll-free 1 888 232 4444)
fax 250 383 6804; email to orders@trafford.com
Book sales in Europe:
Trafford Publishing (UK) Limited, 9 Park End Street, 2nd Floor
Oxford, UK OX1 1HH UNITED KINGDOM
phone 44 (0)1865 722 113 (local rate 0845 230 9601)
facsimile 44 (0)1865 722 868; info.uk@trafford.com
Order online at:
trafford.com/06-0286

10 9 8 7 6 5 4 3 2 1

26. *Brass head of an Oni of Ife, Ife, Nigeria.* *14"*

42 Figure in brass of an Oni of Ife found at Ita Yemoo in 1958. Excavations at the site showed that contemporary terracotta sculptures in a similar style but larger in size had been abandoned by the twelfth century AD. Ife Museum. Ht 18¾ in.

Preface

As a Yorùbá man, I have had two concerns for writing this book: to present Yorùbá grammar in as much depth and variety as possible and to provide framework for understanding them. This volume is intended to contribute to the development of the study of African languages and cultures. It seems to me that this appropriately conceived and well-written material is available for use in both secondary and higher education instructions worldwide. Moreover, it is my hope that this volume will not only be a useful teaching instrument within the formal curriculum, but will also play an important role in shaping the study of African languages in foreign lands.

Previous introductions to African languages and cultures have suffered excessive misconceptions and sweeping generalities, to overcome these problems, I have utilized a series of case studies and juxtaposed particular ethnographic materials. The superb quality of these materials make it possible to present something of general interest in Yorùbá language through analysis of some well-portrayed examples.

ACKNOWLEDGMENT

The writing of this text has been a group effort involving the input and support of my families, friends and colleagues. To each person, I offer my sincere thanks. To begin with, I must cite the contribution of my students who have taken Yoruba courses from me. Students from Albany State University, Darton College, group study students at the Cultural Centers across United States of America, and my interest groups from various churches. It is trite to say that they have a continuing inspiration, and of course, they have. They taught me what students want to know about Yorùbá language and culture.

The quality of a textbook depends greatly on the quality of the prepublication reviews by fellow Yorùbá Professors around the world. In this respect, my first and deepest expression of indebtedness goes to Professor Wande Abimbola of Boston University U.S.A., Professor Wole Soyinka of Emory University in Georgia, for their welcomed advice and encouragements.

A special note of appreciation goes to those colleagues who have taught the Yoruba courses before me at Albany State University in Georgia, the late Professor Samuel Ọládèjì who developed African Studies curriculum, Professor Babátúndé Àbáyòmi, Professor and Dean Abíọ́dún Ọjémákindé, Professor Títí Ọládùnjoyè, Professor and the former Dean James Hill, and Professor Arnold Odio who welcomed the studies of Yorùbá at Albany State University.

There are still fellow professors who have contributed to the development of this book by providing constructive reviews of various portions of the manuscript. Professors Joshua W. Murfree, Jr., Charles Ochie, Babáfémi Èlúfíédè, Samuel Adékúnlé, Engineer Faud Abdullah, Professor Adébísí Fábáyò, Dr. and Mrs. Rex Àjàyí, M.D., Dr. Samuel Rótìmi, Dr. and Mrs. Popezimba, M.D., Professors David Adéwùyì, Olátúndé Òkédìjí, Adansi Amankwaa, Olá Abdullah of Darton College, Mr. and Mrs. Emmanuel Daramola, Dr. and Mrs. Theophilous Àkàndé, Dr. and Mrs. E. Odébùnmi, Mr. Gilbert Udoto, Mr. Edgars Patani, Professor Glenn Zuern and Dr. Títíladé Brito and family.

It is also a pleasure to thank my editors, Mr. James Adédèjì and Matthew Adélékè of Òyó Nigeria who supervised the revision from start to finish with enthusiasm, skill and lots of good ideas. I sincerely appreciate their contributions. If you have suggestions or comments, please feel free to contact me at my e-mail address (aadeleke@aol.com) or aadeleke@asurams.edu.

Albany State University

Albany, Georgia U.S.A.

TABLE OF CONTENTS

Chapter 8	Ẹ̀kọ́ Kejọ	Yorùbá Pronouns

Chapter 9	Ẹ̀kọ́ Kẹsàn	Forming Commands

Chapter 10	Ẹ̀kọ́ Kẹwà	The Yorùbá Food

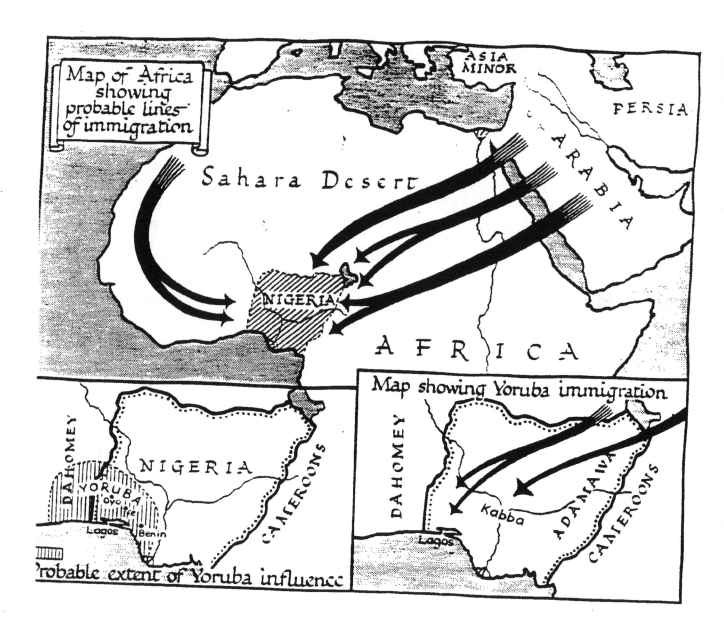

Map of Africa showing probable lines of immigration

Probable extent of Yoruba influence

Map showing Yoruba immigration

Introduction

Yorùbá History and Politics

The Yoruba People, of whom there are over thirty million, mainly live in the southwestern corner of Nigeria along the Dahomey border and extends into the country of Dahomey itself. Also, a growing Disaspora is dispersed around Africa and the world at large. Before the Europeans, i.e., the Portuguese explorers came to the area, the Yorùbá were divided into many independent units that were each ruled by a different king. The king was considered to be a friend of the gods and to have spiritual powers that set him apart from people.

In the fifteenth century, the Portuguese explorers "discovered" the Yorùbá cities and kingdom. However, cities like Ilé-Ifè and Benim City, had been established for at least five hundred years before the Europeans came. According to the archeological evidence, the protoYorùbá (Mok), were residing around the north of the Niger by the first Millennium B.C., and they were then already working with iron.

According to the Ifá theology, human kind arose in the sacred city of Ile-Ife. This is the place Odùduwà (the father of all Yorùbá Kings) created dry land from water. In other words, the Yorùbá believed that the supreme god created the world in the city of Ilé-Ifè, the center for all later Yorùbá Kingdoms. He then sent Odùduwà to Ifè to establish his dynasty. History also revealed that an unknown number of Africans migrated from Mecca to Ilé-Ifè.

Ile-Ife was the first of all Yorùbá cities and it is considered to be the Yorùbá spiritual capitol, perhaps having emerged in the seventh or eight century. The

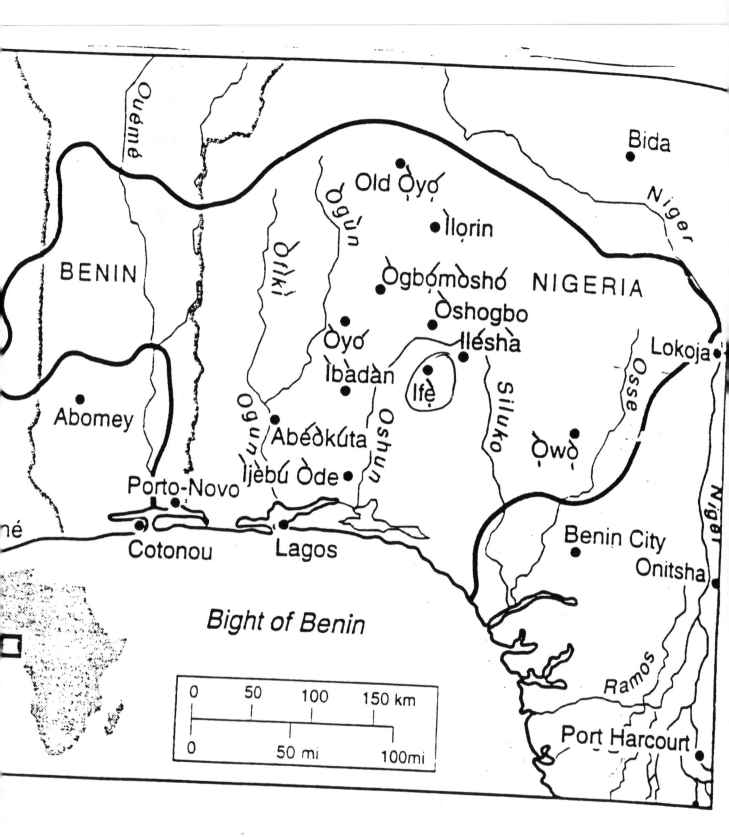

Bida

Old Ọyọ

Ilọrin

BENIN

NIGERIA

Ogbọmoshọ

Oshogbo

Ilesha

Lokoja

Oyọ

Ibadàn

Ifẹ

Abomey

Ọwọ

Abẹokúta

Ijèbú Òde

Porto-Novo

Cotonou

Lagos

Benin City

Onitsha

Bight of Benin

0   50   100   150 km

0   50 mi   100mi

Port Harcourt

Yorùbá traditional ruling families are able to trace their ancestors back to the twelfth century. However, Ilé-Ifè never developed into a true kingdom unlike Òyó and Benin who came later, but grew and expanded as a consequence of their strategic locations at a time when trading became prosperous. Ilé-Ifè remained a city-state and it had paramount importance to the Yorùbá as the original sacred city and the dispenser of basic religious thoughts.

Òyó grew into a great empire, controlling the trade routes linking the sea with the north. In the 18th century, Òyó Empire was torn apart by civil war, collapsing completely in the 1930s. After the demise of Òyó, Ìbàdàn became the most powerful Yorùbá town, controlling a large empire. European slave traders no doubt benefitted from Yorùbá divisions. It is obvious elements of Yorùbá cultural survival and influence spread across the Atlantic to the Americas. European slave hunters violently and forcefully captured and marched several millions of Africans to the Americas and Brazil in the overcrowded slave ships.

Colonialism

As the 19th century progressed, more and more British traders, soldiers, missionaries and government officials entered Yorùbá territory; they were making arrangements with local kings or forcefully stripping power from those who registered, by destroying and looting their towns. The British had established control over the Yorùbás by 1897. The region was incorporated into the protectorate (colony) of Southern Nigeria in 1900.

From 1900 and up an upper class of educated, wealthy business people

3

A SLAVE MARKET

AN ARAB SLAVE RAID

Map showing Slave Routes from Africa.

ATLANTIC OCEAN

EUROPE

ASIA

N TED STATES F MERICA

Turkey

Persia

West Indies

Sahara Desert

Arabia

India

Slave Coast

AFRICA

SOUTH AMERICA

INDIAN OCEAN

SHIPPING SLAVES

developed among the Yorùbá, due to the growth of cocoa and coffee industries. More and more elite among the Yorùbá become involved in local politics. Changes were made to the constitution in 1945 and about ten years later, different parties began to be active, and the struggle against European rule increased.

Nigeria was divided into three regions by the British, the north–where the Hausa-Fulani were most powerful; the southeast–which was Ibo territory; and the southwest–which was the home to the Yorùbás. When Nigeria became independent in 1960, this division brought about ethical and political conflicts. In 1967, the bloody Biafra War broke out after the Ibo tried to separate from the country. As a result, the Yorubas now live in seven states: Òyó, Ògùn, Lagos, Òsun, Kwara, Ondo, and Ewkìtì, instead of one Yorùbá region. The Yorùbás played an important role in Nigeria's gaining independence in 1960. Since then, they have continued to be very important in the country's political life.

Ways of Life

Historically, the Yorùbás are agricultural people, lived in towns that are enclosed by a high wall with the palace of the Oba, marking the central point. Their major agricultural products are yams, cassava, and cocoa.

Central market located at the front of the palace, around it were grouped interconnecting courtyards, houses, and rooms for others to live. In modern times, compounds have largely been replaced by two-story houses, and many obas have built luxurious places.

Taking a quick rank at linguistic or national communities of similar size,

H.M.S. SPEEDY

An early 18th century ship of the British Navy.

THE SIGN OF FREEDOM

EDRISI'S MAP OF AFRICA 1154 A.D. showing incorrect course of the Niger

MUNGO PARK

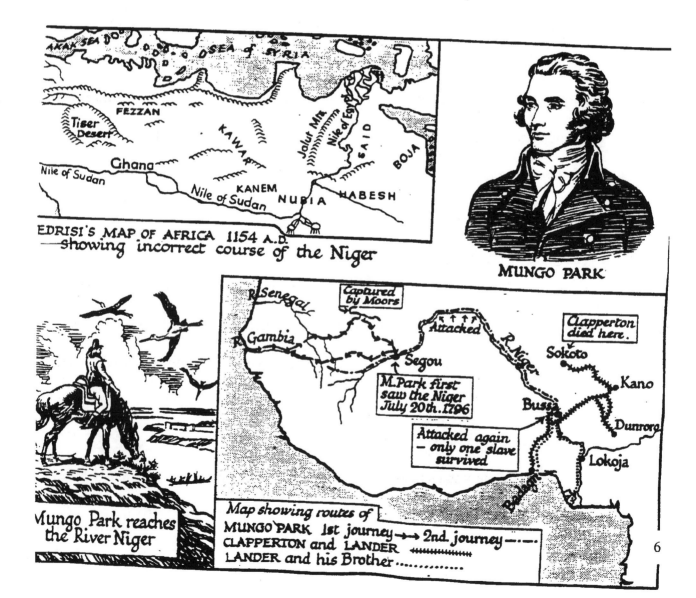

Mungo Park reaches the River Niger

R. Senegal
R. Gambia
Captured by Moors
Attacked
Segou
M. Park first saw the Niger July 20th. 1796
Attacked again — only one slave survived
R. Niger
Clapperton died here.
Sokoto
Kano
Bussa
Dunrora
Lokoja

Map showing routes of
MUNGO PARK 1st journey →→ 2nd journey —.—.
CLAPPERTON and LANDER ++++++++
LANDER and his Brother ....

6

Yorùbá language is roughly equivalent to the total numbers of Dutch language speakers which is (21-30 million), that include Flemish speakers in Belgium. Yorùbá speakers are more than the total population of Australia (18 million today), or the total number of Hungarian speakers (14 million today), or Greek speakers (12 million).

The Yorùbás enjoy common mutually understandable language, despite many dialects and centuries of political and military connection among district city-states and kingdoms. The Yorùbás also pride on the tradition of common origin in the city of Ilé-Ifè and of descends of Odùduwà, the mythical founder of the Yorùbá people.

Yorùbá is a language of scholarship, as well as a major research language in African Studies. As such, it fulfills foreign language requirements in many undergraduate and graduate programs in many universities across the United States and the world at large. The large linguistic beauty of Yorùbá lies not only in its tonal system and the effect it has on the meaning of the words and phrases, but also in the literal meanings derived from such words and phrases.

Moral Characteristics

The Yorùbás are naturally kind and simple hearted people. They are remarkably courteous in their mutual exchange, and strongly attached to their country, friends and kindred. All their moral virtues, and especially gratitude and honesty, are reflected in their proverbs, myths, legends, fables, oral traditions, poetries and idiomatic expressions.

Adultery and domestic violence are rarer than one could imagine. There are

Nicon Noga Hilton Hotel
ABUJA, NIGERIA

hardly cases of illegitimate children. However, their custom that allow men to marry more than one woman (polygamy) may be strange, yet these polygamous families are strongly bonded together as a nucleus family unit, even more bonded to each other than "step parenting." The Yorubas are well recognized among civilized nations.

Establishment of Ọyọ

Ọyọ́ was established by Ọrànmíyàn, the last born son of Odùduwà. Ọrànmíyàn was very powerful, very active and a renounced warrior. He vowed that he would seek revenge on the circumstances that surrounded the death of his father Lámúrúdu, from people of Mecca. With this courage, he went to Mecca to wage war against his father's enemies. However, there was an instruction from the Ifá oracle that as he goes, he must stop wherever he comes across a large python (snake) in his journey. He was instructed to settle on the very spot because he will be abundantly blessed there. As ọrànmíyàn approached river Niger near Minna, he saw a large python snake, he did not do otherwise, he just established the first Àafín there. He acquired extensive acres of land from Bàríbá division to the Tapa land.

From the onset, the Ọyọ́ people were being called the Yorùbás. However, when the white missionaries came to the Yorùbá land in 1843, they were encouraged to address all the Yorùbá speaking citizens as Yorùbás, just as we do today. Before the missionaries arrived, all tribes of Yorùbá were scattered all over without tribal identity. For example, the Èkìtì, Ẹgbá, Ìjẹbú, and so on.

The Aláafin is being referred to as the King of the Land of Ọyọ́-Yorùbá. Although other cities have kings that rule their people, however, these kings always

LAGOS / NIGERIA
Ikoyi Hotel

give honor and high homage to the Aláàfin. After the Ọ̀yọ́ Ilé was conquered in the Fúláǹi War, Àgọ́ Dọ̀yọ́ was established and this is where the new Ọ̀yọ́ is situated and this is the Ọ̀yọ́ town where the Aláàfin reigns today.

Among the Ọ̀yọ́-Yorùbá are people from Òkè-Ògùn, whose dialects are a little different from the Ọ̀yọ́ proper. Also, the Ọ̀yọ́-Yorùbá include the people from Ọ̀yọ́ Township, Ilé-Ifẹ̀, Òshogbo, Ìbàdàn and other major cities in the Ọ̀yọ́-Yorùbá are Ọ̀yọ́, Ògbómọ̀shọ, Ìsẹ́yìn, Ẹde, Ìwó, the Ìbàràpá division such as Igbó-Ọra, Èrúwà and Làǹláte. Among the kings (Ọba) in the Yorùbá land include the Ọ̀ọ̀ni of Ifẹ̀, Aláàfin of Ọ̀yọ́, Olúbàdàn of Ìbàdàn, Àtáója of Òshogbo, Timì of Ẹde, Sòun of Ògbómọ̀shọ, Asẹ́yìn of Ìsẹ́yìn, Olúwò of Ìwó, and Emir of Ìllọrin.

The Ìgbómìnà division is also important among the Yoruba tribes. There is Ìjẹbú Òde, Ìjẹ̀bú-Igbó, Ìjẹ̀bú-Rẹmo, Ìjẹ̀bú-Ìjárí, Ìjẹbú, "esè odò" at the riverside. Among the crowned kings of Ijẹbu land are the Aùjalè, Àkárigbò and Orímolúsì (Ọba Ìjèbúigó). The Ìjẹ̀bús have different dialects, however, they understand each other very well.

The Ìjẹ̀shà are another tribe of the Yorùbá land. Among their big cities are Iléshà, Ìjẹ̀búJèshà, Ìpetu-Jèshà, Ibòkùn, and Ẹsà-Òkè. Ekìtì dialect is one of the dialects that is similar to that of Ìjẹ̀shà. Among the big cities in Èkìtì are Adó-Ekìtì, Ìdó, Ìkẹ́rẹ́, Ikòlé, Ifaki, and Ijero. Their kings are titled, Ajérò of Ìjerò Èkìtì, Ẹlékòlé of Ikòlé, and Èwi of Adó and so on.

After these, we will find the cities called Àkúré, Oǹdó, Ìlàjẹ, and Ìkàlé. They have different dialects but all of them understand each other. The Ẹ̀gbás and the

1. Guardian figure of wood and copper, Bakota tribe. Congo region. 2. Wooden statue of high-ranking person, Basundi tribe, Lower Congo. 3. Head from wooden figurine of Baule tribe, Guinea Coast. 4. Wooden hippopotamus from the Barotse tribe, Zambia. 5. Copper guardian figure to protect tombs, Bakota tribe, Congo. 6. Wooden bird, probably a hornbill, about 4 feet high, Senufo tribe, Ivory Coast.

Ẹgbádòs are important tribes among the children of Yorùbá. Abéòkúta, Ilaròo, Ayétán, Ìmẹ̀kọ and Ifọ̀ are their major cities. Aláké is the head of the kings in Ẹ̀gbá land. Facial marks are common among the Ẹ̀gbádò just like that of other Ọ̀yọ́-Yorùbás.

The Àwóris and Ègùns are closer to the riverside. Although both dialects are similar, they are difficult to understand like other Yorùbá tribes. They have a lot to do with the Yorùbá at Kétu in the country of Dahomey, Sábèe, and Pópó in the country of Togo.

Other Yorùbá tribes include Àkókó, Ọ̀wọ̀, Ifọ̀n and Binni. Dialects are very difficult to understand around here; it is even difficult for the Akókó people to understand Ọ̀wọ̀ people.

As many as the Yorùbá tribes and dialects, it is amazing that the proper Yorùbá-Ọ̀yọ serves as the medium of communication among all the Yorùbás. Yorùbá-Ọ̀yọ is the only recognized "written form" language among all the Yorùbá dialects. We write and read it in books; we use it for news and official communication. Yorùbá-Ọ̀yọ is the language of education in the schools. Therefore, the Yorùbás are proud about their ability to speak two Yorùbá languages the Yorùbá proper and the Yorùbá dialects.

There are rich heritage literature and poetries written in Yorùbá. For example, the playwright Dúró-Làdiépọ̀ and Albert Ògúndé are two examples of well known playwrights in the Yorùbá language. Yorùbá has a rich oral literature that they pass from generation to generation. In fact, their sense of unity has been

13

University of Lagos
Senate and Administration Buildings

connected to their language and culture, rather than to politics.

How Yorùbá Language Came into Written Form

In the 1500s, the European slave traders arrived on African soil to capture young men and women into slavery. However, in 1807, the British government attempted to eradicate and abolish slave trade. For this reason, the British government, established a nation in the West African Coast named Sierra Leone. Freetown, in Sierra Leone, was established for the freed slaves to live since millions of the captured slaves could no longer trace their way back to their original ancestors. All the captured slaves in 1807 were sent back to Freetown the capital city by the British Coast Guards for protection and freedom.

The Church Missionary Society (C.M.S.) Anglican in Britain sent missionaries to Sierra Leone, to propagate the gospel of Jesus Christ among the freed slaves. Among these missionaries are John Raban, Clapperton, and Mrs. Hannah Kilhan. These missionaries worked hard to make sure the Yorùbá language get into written form so that it will be easier for the Yorùbá people to translate the Bible into Yorùbá language. One of the first freed slaves was Bishop Samuel Àjàyí Crowther and Andrew Wilhelm. Crowther was very dedicated to the work of missions, especially in translating the Holy Bible from English language into Yorùbá. The task of writing the Yorùbá language down started in Freetown. In 1850, Bishop Samuel Àjàyí Crowther with M. Raban and J. Schon (missionaries) arrived at Abéòkúta (Ògùn State today) to research how Yorùbá language can be lettered.

Missionaries Raban and Schon both from Germany searched for the Yorùbá

BÍṢǪ̀ǪBÙ / BISHOP SAMUEL ÀJÀYÍ

Samuel Àjàyí Crowther, the first student of Fourah Bay College, Sierra Leone, was born at Òsògùn a few kilometers south of Iséyìn. He was kidnapped by slave traders in 1821, rescued a year later and became a mission school boy in 1823. He had a brilliant college career (1828) and became a clergyman (1843)

He distinguished himself in such areas as evangelism, crusade against slave trade and education (translation of Prayer Book into Yorùbá, authored grammar books for Yorùbá, Ibo and Nupe languages), medicine and architecture.

He died on 1st December 1891.
(Federal Ministry of Information, Nigeria)
(Ilé-iṣẹ́ aláṣẹ fún Ìkéde Ìròhìn Ìjọba àpapọ̀, Nàìjíríà)

16

alphabet (A, B, D). Àjàyí Crowther was a big help to these missionaries, he made sure that both vowels and consonants of the Yorùbá language were complete. Àjàyí supplied the three tones that enables us to differentiate the high, flat and low tones in the Yorùbá language.

In 1840, some freed Yorùbá slaves decided to go back to their father's land. For this reason, Missionary Henry Townsend took them back from Sierra Leone to Abéòkuta, with a Yorùbá ex-slave man called Andrew Wilhelm. After a while, Missionary Henry Townsend left for Abéòkuta for Sierra Leone, but left Andrew Wilhelm at Abéòkúta. Both Andrew and Samuel were at Abeokúta. By 1843, Samuel had acquired a tremendous skill in translation and he was readily available to do the job very well. In 1856-1862, he translated the Lord's Prayer, the Decalogue and the Gospel according to St. Matthew into Yorùbá. In addition, he translated the local Christian English Newspaper into Yorùbá. Townsend started the Christian Newspaper between 1859-1867 in Àbéòkúta.

Under the leadership of Àjàyí Crowther, the missionaries were able to accomplish a whole lot of progress in getting Yorùbá into a written form. The translation of the Holy Bible from English into Yorùba started in 1854 and this translation was completed in 1880. After these, he was able to work on the hymn books, service books and the New Testament in 1848-1849, while the Old Testament was translated between 1850-1856. The proper Yorùbá-Òyọ́ is the language of the Yorùbá Bible, service books and hymn books. This is an agreement with all the ministers of the gospel because Yorùbá Òyọ́ is the deepest and the easiest to

Dakar: Vue de la Banque Central et l'Ile de Gorée
Dakar: View on the Central Bank and the Goree Island
Dakar: Ansicht auf die Zentralbank und die Goree-Insel

understand to all Yorùbàs. Eventually, schools were built by the missionaries and when children attended the Christian schools, they automatically became Christians. Hospitals were also established by the missionaries, both education and medical facilities were very persuasive to many people, thus Christianity became popular and converts were increasing. Among the first Mission Schools and churches established in 1844 are St. David's Church, School at Kudetì, Ìbàdàn Nigeria, and St. Andrew College, Ọyọ.

Yorùbá Religious Beliefs

All the Yorùbá people believe in one universal God, the creator and preserver of all things, whom they generally call Ọlọrun (o li ọrun), the Owner or Lord of Heaven, and sometimes by other names, as Olódùmarè, the Ever-Righteous, Ọgá-Ògo, Glorious High One, Olúwa, Lord. They hold the doctrines of imortality of the soul and of future rewards and punishments, but on these points their notions are obscure. All the dead are in ọrun Hades. Oke-ọrun, the Upper Hades, is the abode of the righteous, and Ọrun-àpadì, the Crucible-Hades, is the place of punishment.

The idols are never confounded with God, either in name or character. They are called orisa, a name which appears to be derived from àsà, customs, or religious ceremonies. Among the numerous òrìsàs worshiped, there are three great ones, called Ọbàtálá, Shàngó, and Ifa. Ọbàtála is thought to be the first made and greatest of all created things. Others, however, affirm that he was nothing more than an ancient king of Yorùbá, and they profess to tell the name of his father. His name Obàtálá appears to be a contraction of ọba ti ńla, the king who is great, or of ọba ti

19

COULEURS DU SENEGAL
1013 - DAKAR : Vue Aenenne
La place de l'Independance et l'hotel TERANGA / Photo M. RENAUDEAU

àlà, the king of whiteness, i.e., purity. A white cloth (ala) is worn by his worshipers. Some of his other names are, Òrìsà ńlá, the great orisa; Alàmòrére', he of the good clay, because he made the human body of clay; and Orisa Popo, the orisa of the gate, because he is the guardian of the gates of cities. He is frequently represented as a warrior on horseback, holding a spear. His wife, Ìyáńgbà, the receiving mother, is represented as a nursing child. But Iyangba herself is Ọbàtálà. The two are one, or in other words, Ọbàtala is an androgyne, representing the productive energy of nature as distinguished from the creative power of God. Ọbàtálà forms or produces the bodies of men; but God himself imparts life and spirit, and God alone is styled Eledá, Creator. The second great òrìsà is Shàngó, the thunder god, who is also called Jákúta, the Stone-caster. The stones or thunderbolts which Sàngó casts down from heaven are preserved as sacred relics. In appearance they are identical with the so-called stone-hatchets picked up in fields of America; but whether they are made originally for battle axes, or leather dressing implements, or emblematic thunderbolts, is not easily determined.

According to one account, Shàngó was born at Ifè, and reigned at Kòso, a town recently destroyed which stood thirty or forty miles south of Shaki. He was much addicted to predatory wars, in commemoration of which his worshipers still carry a bag, as the emblem of booty. When a house is truck by lightening, they have a right to pillage it, and also to steal as many goats and chickens as they can find at large in any part of the town. They affirm that their master was translated alive into heaven, where he reigns in great state, having a place with gates of brass, and ten

21

94 Wooden figure from the Shongo shrine of the King of
Oyo at Koso. Its name is *ere Alafin Shongo*, carving of or for
King Shongo, who was one of the first kings of Oyo and who
has since become identified with thunder and lightning.
According to Philip Allison, who collected this piece, such a
figure used to be made for each new king who visited the
shrine at Koso at an early stage in his installation ceremonies,
where he was crowned with a cloth crown which was left
behind on one of the figures in the shrine. The king is never
allowed to visit the shrine again. This figure is said to have
been brought in 1837 from Koso at Old Oyo to the new site
of Koso. Nigerian Museum, Lagos. Ht 38 in.

thousand horses, and amusing himself with hunting, fishing and war.

But the abstract Sàngó is quite a different being. He is the son of Ọrungàn, midday and the grandson of Aginjù, the desert. His mother is Yemọja, the mother of fishes, a small river in Yoruba land. His elder brother is Dàda, nature, one of the Yorùbá idols; his younger brother is the river Ògùn, which bears the name of the God of War and Smith's work. His wives are the rivers Ọya, Ọsun, and Ọbà; his associate is Òrìsáko, the god of farms, his slave is Biri, darkness; and his priest is Màgbà, the receiver.

The third great idol is Ifá, the revealer of future events, and the patron of marriage and childbirth. He is called Bàngà, the god of palmnuts because sixteen palm-nuts are employed in obtaining responses. The head-quarters of Ifá are at Adó, a village on the top of an immerse rock near Awaye.

There are several other idols of note, as Odududa, the universe, located at Ifè; Dàda nature, and Òrisaoko, the god of farms, whose symbol is a large iron bar. These bars are obtained at a great cost from the high priest of idol, who dwells at Ìràwò. Many of the inferior idols are men and women who were distinguished in their day by some remarkable relation to the tribe.

The doctrine of idolatry prevalent in Yorùbá land appears to be derived by analogy from the form and customs of the civil government. There is but one king in the nation, and one God over the universe. Petitioners to the king approach him through the intervention of his servants, courtiers, and nobles; and the petitioner conciliates the courtier whom he employs good words and presents. In like manner

Agura Hotel
Abuja, Nigeria

24

Yoruba Complete Female Dressing

Mrs Obasanjo reading her address at the Women Luncheon at the RPC/CEF conference in Chicago.

NIGERIA'S GLAMOROUS FIRST LADY, CHIEF (MRS) STELLA OBASANJO RECEIVES A PRESTIGIOUS AWARD IN AMERICA FOR HER CARE FOR THE UNDERPRIVILEGED CHILDREN OF NIGERIA

Pix by Beverly Swanagan in Chicago

For Chief Mrs Stella Obasanjo, Nigeria's first lady, it was yet another day of glory in a foreign land. Recently, The Rainbow Coalition, led by Reverend Jesse Jackson Honoured her at a prestigious ceremony in Chicago, U.S.A. She got the Award for her pet project, The Child Care Trust. In recent years Chief Mrs Obasanjo had received many laurels and accolades for her love of and support for the under privileged child.

OVATION brings you exclusive pictures from the colourful event which was attended by American former President, Bill Clinton and a host of other supporters of good cause from far and near.

no man can directly approach God; but the Almighty himself, they say, has appointed various kinds of orisas, who are mediators and intercessors between himself and mankind. No sacrifices are made to God, because he needs nothing; but the orisas, being much like men, are pleased with offerings of sheep, pigeons, and other things. They conciliate the orisa, or mediator, that he may bless them not in his own power, but in the power of God.

As the people make clear distinction between God and idols, so an idol, which is a real spiritual being, is not to be confounded with its symbol, *which may be an image, a tree, or a stone, a charm or amulet is thought to have much power, but it is not an orisa. It has no life and no intelligence as the orisas have. White men are generally much mistaken in regard to the religion and superstition of the Yorùbás. They suppose that the idols are looked upon as gods; that the symbol is the idol; and that a greegree, or charm, is an object of worship–all of which is incorrect.

It is usual among Europeans to call the idols of the natives "devils." The natives themselves speak of only one devil, though they believe in the existence of various other evil spirits. In the Yorùbá language the devil is called Esu, the Ejected, from sù, to cast out; and Elégbarà, the Mighty, on account of his great influence over mankind. The name Ebilisi has been borrowed from the Pulohs, and by them from the Arabs. The devil is not reckoned as one of the mediatorial orisas; but the Yorùbás worship him with sacrifices, to conciliate his favor and prevent his doing them injury.

Egungun, bones, and Orò, torment, are the executive or vindictive power of

226 Panel from a door carved by Arowogun. Nigerian Museum, Lagos. W. 25 in.

227 Panel from a door carved by Oshamuko, former apprentice of Arowogun. Nigerian Museum, Lagos. Ht of panel: $14\frac{1}{4}$ in.

civil government deified. The latter is most usual among the Egbas, who term the punishment of criminals "giving them to Orð." On Orð day, all women are obliged to remain closely shut up in their houses. Egúngún, or the "Aku Devil," makes his appearance in the person of a tall fellow, fantastically clad and masked, and is declared to be a tenant of the grave. No one, not even the king, may dare to lay his hand on Egungun; and if any man should say he is a man, she would be put to death. Even Mohamedans and Christians are obliged to conceal their knowledge of the imposture under penalty of martyrdom.

Exercise

1. Why were the missionaries interested in getting Yorubá language into a written form?

2. What is the importance of Abèokuta in the development of Yorùbá language?

3. Write all you know about Samuel Àjàyí Crowther.

4. Discuss how Yorubá language got into written form.

5. List all the Yorùbà Gods you know. Then briefly compare them with the Christian God.

6. Which of the Yorùbà idols is most interesting to you. Explain.

7. Name ten major cities in the Yoruba land.

8. Name ten kings' titles and its cities they rule.

9. What was the importance of Freetown?

10. Name five great abolitionist and summarize their activities.

Christ Church Cathedral
Lagos, Nigeria

The Yorùbá alphabet consists of twenty-five letters, that include, seven vowels and eighteen consonants. Both the alphabet, vowels and the consonants are as follows:

Aa   Bb   Dd   Ee   Ẹẹ

Ff   Gg   Gbgb   Hh   Ii

Jj   Kk   Ll   Mm   Nn

Oo   Ọọ   Pp   Rr   Ss

Ṣṣ   Tt   Uu   Ww   Yy

THE YORUBA ALPHABET

A àga = chair	**B** bàtà = shoe	**D** dùrù = organ (musical)	**E** ewé = leaf/lea	**E** eiye = bird
F fìlà = cap (hat)	**G** garawa = pail	**Gb** gbòngbò = root	**H** ehín = tooth	**I** ìwé = book
J jígí = mirror	**K** kèké = bicycle	**L** labalábá = butterfly	**M** màlúù = cow	**N** Nàìjíríà = Nigeria
O owó = money	**O** ògèdè = banana	**P** pupa = red	**R** ràkúnmí = camel	**S** sálúbàtà = sandal(s)
S sòkòtò = pants/trousers	**T** tòlótóló = turkey	**U** dúdú = black	**W** wàrà = milk	**Y** yàrá = room (inside house)

32

Pronunciation of the Alphabet

(Bia se npe awon alifabeti ni yi)

A as in Ah	B as in Bee	D as in Dee
E as in Eh	Ẹ as in Ẹf	F as in Fi
G as in Gill	Gb as in gb	H as in Hill
I as in heel	J as in jee	K as in kee
L as in Lee	M as in me	N as in nee
O as in Oo	Ọ as in Or	P as in PP
R as in Re	S as in See	Ṣ as in She
T as in Tee	U as in Hood	W as in We
Y as in Yield		

Compared to English, there is no:

Cc, Qq, Vv, Xx, Zz

But we have:

Ẹẹ, Gbgb, Ọọ, Ṣṣ

Vowels and Consonants:

1. Àwon Fáwéèlì ti kii see Àranmúpè - The non-nasalized oral vowels Aa, Ee, Ẹẹ, Ii, Oo, Ọọ, Uu

2. Àwón Faweli Àranmúpè - Nasalized vowels by adding 'n' to an oral vowel symbol (i.e) Ọn/an, ẹn, in, un.

THE YORUBA ALPHABET

A arm a-pá	**B** shoe Bata	**D** sword Dòjé	**E** teeth Ehín	**Ẹ** bird Ẹiyẹ
F hat Fila	**G** pail Garawa	**Gb** root Gbòngbò	**H** back ẹ hin	**I** tree Igi
J mirror Jigi	**K** bike Kẹkẹ	**L** butterfly Labalaba	**M** cow Màlù	**N** relaxing Najú
O money Owó	**Ọ** hand ọwọ	**P** duck pẹpẹyẹ	**R** camel ràkúnmi	**S** sandal salubata
Ṣ church sọsi	**T** turkey tolotaló	**U** uhaul uhaul	**W** milk wara	**Y** mosquito yanmuyámú

Vowels (Simple Vowels)

The non-nasalized oral Yorùbá vowels.

There are seven vowels in the Yorùbá alphabet as shown below:

Aa   Ee   Ẹẹ   Ii   Oo   Ọọ   Uu

The pronunciation of each goes thus:

Compare these oral vowels in Yorùbá with English and see how close they are in sound:

[a] as in àga _____chair

[e] as in ejò_____snake

[e] as in ẹkó_____education

[I] as in igi_____tree

[o] as in okùn_____rope

[o] as in Ọrúnlá_____dried okra

[u] as in ùgù_____vegetable

Write and practice the pronunciation of ten consonants with any vowel from "a" to "y". Many of these are prefixes of words, because they have no meanings.

Examples: Read Horizontally

Ba	da	ba	fa	pa	ra	sa	ya	ta	ma
Be	de	be	fe	pe	re	se	ye	te	me
Be	de	be	fe	pe	re	se	ye	te	me
Bi	di	vi	fi	pi	ri	si	yi	ti	mi
Bo	do	bo	fo	po	ro	so	yo	to	mo

The Author Conducts National Anthem

The Nigerian Boy Scouts

Bo	do	bo	fo	po	ro	so	yo	to	mo
Bu	du	bu	fu	pu	ru	su	yu	tu	mu, etc.

Nasalized vowels are formatted by adding an "n" to an oral vowel symbol.

The use of nasalized vowels

in	an	on	un
Oyin (honey)	ìyàn (famine)	ìpọ́n (file)	ikùn-buggar in nose – imú
ìyìn (praise)	ìyán (yarn)	ìbon (gun)	ikùn-stomach
ẹyin (egg)	iyán (pounded Yam)	àgbọn (cocunut)	òkun-sea/beach

Elision of Vowels

Most Yoruba verbs end in a vowel either pure or nasal. Examples:

> Pa - to kill
>
> Pè - to call
>
> Se - to do
>
> Rà - to buy

However, most of the nouns begin with vowel; examples:

> Àga - Chair
>
> Owó - Money
>
> Àtùpà - Lamb

To save time, it is necessary while speaking, to drop either the final vowel of the verb or the initial noun that follows it. In other words, when two vowels of the

37

Mrs Dayo Keshi

A Look of Hope

same meaning concur, one of them is dropped. For example, see everyday conversations below.

Everyday Conversation

	Without Elision	**With Elision**
1.	Mo fé mu omi/	Mo fé mu 'mi/
	I want to drink water	I want to drink water
2.	Mó fé je eran/	Mo fé jeran/
	I want to eat some meat	I want to eat some meat
3.	Mo fé lo sí ilé/	Mo fé lo 'lé/
	I want to go home	I want to go home
4.	Si ilekùn/open the door	Si'lekun/open the door.
5.	Bi ila - give room	B'ila/give room
6.	Ba eru - fearful	B'eru/fearful
7.	Je ifa - cheat	Je 'fa/cheat
8.	Fi ìjà bí-born during conflicts	Fi 'ja bí/born during conflicts

Assimilation of Vowels

Assimilation is either perfect of imperfect. In perfect assimilation, the unaccented "o" becomes identical with the accented vowel for the word to which it is appended.

YORUBA SHANGO PEDESTAL

40

The objective pronoun of the third person is regularly exchanged for the vowel which is identical with the governing verb, that is, the pronoun assumes all the following forms:

Èmi mà án/I know him/her

Èmi bẹ̀ẹ́/I begged him/her

Èmi yìn ín/I praised him/her

Èmi pè é/I called him/her

Èmi fẹ́ẹ́/I love him/her

Èmi rí i/I saw him/her

The principle applies equally when the governing word is a preposition, as:

Báa - with him/her/mo báa lọ/I went with him/her

Síi - to him/her/mo kọwé síi/I wrote him/her

Fún un - for him/her/mo korin fún un/I sang for him/her

> Nasalized vowels are formed by adding an "n" to an oral vowel symbol, except where such a symbol "id" preceded by an "m" or "n".

> Nasalized vowels can stand for a third person singular pronoun that is the object following a verb having a nasalized vowel.

Examples:

Yìn ín/praising him or her

Muún tán/drink it all

Rá an pá/to sew it up

Fún un je/give it to him to eat

Atiku Abubakar and Mrs Dayo Keshi

42

Gbọ ọn nù dádá/shake it up real well

Nàán sun kún/beat him or her until he/she cries

Kùn uń dádá/paint it real well

Pin in fún won/divide it for them

Sàn án tán/paid it all

Pòọn tit ti yio fi sùn/carry the baby on the back until he or she sleeps

<u>Exercise</u>

1. How many Alphabets do we have in Yorùbá language?

2. Write all the alphabet in upper case form.

3. What is the fifth alphabet in the Yorùbá language?

4. What is the last alphabet in the Yorùbá language?

5. What alphabet appears twice, differentiated by dots at the bottom?

6. Which letters are missing in the Yorùbá Alphabet that we use in the English alphabet?

7. Write the entire twenty-five alphabets in lower case form.

8. How many vowels do we have in the Yorùbá alphabet?

9. What are the five examples of nasalized vowels?

10. What is the difference between non-nasalized and nasalized vowels?

11. Use vowel: a, e, ẹ, i, o, ọ and u to form prefix words.

12. Differentiate between a vowel and a consonant.

13. How many consonants do we have in the Yorùbá alphabet?

14. List the prefix that can go with the consonants before a word can be formed: b, g, f, gb, h, k, l, m, n and p.

CORPORATE NIGERIANS GATHER FOR THE FABULOUS PRESENTATION OF THE NEW **BMW 7-SERIES** IN LAGOS

By Tosan Aduayi and Ajayi Oyebo

15. (a) List five words with elision. (b) List five words without elision.

CONSONANTS

There are eighteen consonants in the Yoruba alphabet. They are: b, d, f, g, gb, h, j, k, l, m, n, p, r, s, s, t, w, y.

If any vowel is added after each of them, it forms a word or may form a verb each.

1. Some may form real words, prefix of a word or suffix of another or just meaningless.

Look at the following examples: Read horizontally.

Bá - touch	Bú - crack	Dù - struggle
Be - prefix of a verb (no meaning)	Dá - break	Fà - pull
Bẹ́ - jump	Dé - arrive	Ga - tall
Bí - deliver a baby	Dẹ̀ - soft	Ré - cut
Bò - cover	Dí - block	Fẹ́ - like
Bọ́ - drop	Rà - buy	Sè - cook

2. If a vowel is added before and after the consonant, it forms a full word, for example:

46

YORÙBÁ BEADED CROWN

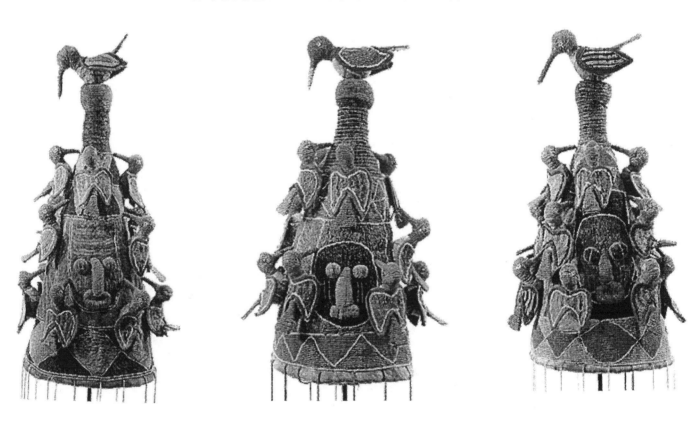

YORÙBÁ, BEADED CROWN 4, Nigeria, 21", $600, © Tim Hamill

Worn by the king, or Oba, in public ceremonies, they are embellished with symbolic designs. Beads were signs of wealth and status. The veil, here incomplete, separated the divine king from mortals. It has 11 strands, averaging 10" long. The opposite side of the crown is similar, with a face and more attached birds.

a	b	d	e
a-j-á – dog	I-b-à – fever	a-d-é – crown	è-r-è – profit reward
a-r-a – body	ọ-b-ọ – monkey	e-d-é – lobster	è-s-ó – fashion

e	f	g	gb
ẹpà – peanut	ifé – love	àgó – hut	egbé – society
ẹwà – black eye pea	ọfé – free	ọgá – boss	àgbá – drum

h	l	j	k
ẹhìn – back	ìjà – fight	ojo – coward	ẹka – branch
ehin – teeth			

The BMW pose

Blessed Memory

48

Chigozie Obi Nnadozie and Gloria Gbalekuma

Yorùbá is a tonal language, accents must be placed on the words for correct punctuation.

<u>Types of Syllables</u>

1.   Mono-syllables

2.   Dy-syllables

3.   Multi-syllables/triple

Mono-syllables are syllables with one accent (or) no accent; for example:

Ké -- cut	gbà – here take
Rà – buy	pọ̀n – carry the baby
Mì – swallow	kó – collect
Pa – kill	fa – pull
Je – eat	gùn – climb
Dó – to have sex	bè – beg
Fẹ́ – like	yan – fry
Kú – die	bé – jump
Dú – struggle	dè – tie
Tì – push	mu – drink
Rán – sew	Ko – write
fin – Carve	kí – geet
wọ̀ – wear	

Yoruba, Nigeria

Bracelet with leopard image. The Benin kingdom was founded by the son of an Ife king in the early 14th century AD. The art of bronze casting was introduced to Benin around the year 1280. Leopard images have been identified with King Ewuare. Tradition maintained that one day as he was sleeping underneath a tree, a leopard lying on one of its upper branches dripped blood down on him. On waking Ewuare killed the leopard and began a yearly tradition of sacrificing leopards to promote royal destiny. The danger and quickness of the leopard served as a potent metaphor for royal power, Benin kings often being referred to as "leopards of the house." Leopard teeth and pelts were given by Benin monarchs to important chiefs and military leaders under their command. This bracelet with the image of leopard has a symbolic meaning in some ceremonies of the Yoruba people.

Material: bronze or brass

Size: H. 8", W. 4 ½"

Poly/dy-syllables are syllables with two accents and tones, for example:

bàbá – father		ìyá – mother
gèlè – head scarf		ọmọ – baby
ìgbà – time		òrọ – word
àsè – feast		ìwo – horn
àsà – custom		ìkà – mean/wicked
àpà – vanderlistic		ìwọ – hook
bàtá – shoe		abà – village
bàrà – the king's burial ground		ejò-snake
bèbè – bank of river		oko – farm
bùbá – the top ware of the ladies outfit		ayọ̀ – joy
ìró – the rap cloth		eran – animal
emu – palm wine		aṣọ – cloth
ìmò – knowledge		ojo – coward
àwò – color		òjò – rain
gbèsè – debt		ara – body
ìwé – book		gbogbo – all
aya – wife		iyọ̀ – salt
omi – water		ata – pepper
isu – yam		pupa – red
epo – oil		ení – mat
agò – stupidity		ìwà – character

52

Dancer of the *gelede* society of Meko in western Yorubaland. The dances are intended to placate the witches in the community by entertaining them. The superstructures add to the entertainment value of the mask: this one represents a couple riding a motorcycle. The eye of the mask resembles those on Nok sculptures; the pierced pupil is not intended for looking through, as can be seen, for the dancer's eye is visible below the mask. The colourful costume makes effective use of imported plastic materials.

ẹ̀bùn – gift   agbo – audience

dòdò – fried plantain   asọ̀ – murmur

funfun – white   pàsán – whip

fẹ́ràn – to love   ọkọ̀ – motor car

dúdú – black and shine   àrà – wonder

Multi/triple syllables with three or more tones, for example:

Àjàgbé (name)   Akúsẹ́ – a poor person

Àdúkẹ́ (name)   Ìjòyè – a chief

Àbèbí (name)   Òkànbí – the lone –

                                      child

Àlàbá (name)   Ògèdẹ̀ – banana

Àwẹ̀ní (name)   Kóríko – grass

Tones

1) High Tone (mi mi)	2) Low Tone (do do)
ómọ́ – it's clean (sounds mimi)	dùrù – organ (sound do do)
ódé – arrives	ẹ̀pà – peanut
kíké – name	bàtà – shoe
mímọ́ – holy	fìlà – hat
títí – name	kòmọ̀ – it/he/she/didn't know

3) Middle Tone (re re) no accent lines	
rere – goodness	ara – body

YORUBA, BEADED FIGURES 20, Nigeria, 32", $800, © Tim Hamill

Beads were signs of wealth and status. Many Yorùbá sacred and secular objects were embellished with elaborate images and symbolic designs created by small glass beads.

eja – fish

isu – yam

ọmọ – baby

igi – tree

ore – gift

ẹyẹ – bird

aṣa – rude

lóyún – get pregnant

4) Combination or Multiple Syllables With Tones

1. Àgbàà gbà – The elderly ones

2. Kábíyèsí – your highness

3. Álágbára – strong person

4. Onísòwò – a trader

5. Àmúlùmólà – mixture

6. Àgídìgbó – musical instrument

7. Pàjáwìrì – in a hurry

8. Ògínníntìn – cold season

9. Pátápátá – in its entirety

10. Porongodo – all gone

11. Kúkúúndùkú – sweet potato

12. Jegúdújerá – vandalistic

13. Kàrángídá – it's amazing

14. Alákitiyan – a very active person/industrious

15. Àgbàlagba – a very old person

16. Àgádágodo – key

17. Pòpòndó – an African bean

56

YORUBA BEADWORK

YORUBA, BEADED MATERNITY GROUP, Nigeria, 21", $500, © Tim Hamill

Beads were signs of wealth and status. Many Yorùbá sacred and secular objects were embellished with elaborate images and symbolic designs created by small glass beads.

18. Ọpalambá – a broken bottle

19. Akerengbe – gourd

20. Lakanlaka – heaping

21. Alarekereke – trickish/dubious

22. Pagidan – it's a purity

23. Alagbawi – defender/lawyer

24. Papajaja – emergency

25. Alupayida – miraculous

26. Aginju – wilderness/desert

27. Pakanleke – trouble prone

28. Adabanija – easier said than done

29. Alujannu – monster

30. Karangida – baffles

31. Tembelekun – malice

32. Agalamasa – kind of bird

33. Alakitiyan – active

34. Alaseju – greedy

35. Alagbede – blacksmith

36. Ọperekete – palm tree

37. Polongo – proclaim

38. Kekereawo – a big man in small status

39. Kekerenke – cock crow

YORÙBÁ BEADWORK

YORUBA, BEADED BOTTLE 19, Nigeria, 12", $400, © Tim Hamill

This beaded bottle has a beaded bird stopper. Beads were signs of wealth and status. Many Yorùbá sacred and secular objects were embellished with elaborate images and symbolic designs created by small glass beads.

40. Ogúnlógò – plenty/multitude

Exercise

1. List five examples of high-tones in:

    a. Mono-syllables

    b. Dy-syllables

    c. Triple syllables

2. List five examples of mid-tones in:

    a. Mono-syllables

    b. Dy-syllables

    c. Triple syllables

3. List five examples of low-tones in:

    a. Mono-syllables

    b. Dy-syllables

    c. Triple syllables

4. Supply the correct tone for the following words:

    a. Labalábá – butterfly

    b. Ògèdè – banana

    c. Wàrà – milk

    d. Dúdú – black

    e. Tòlótóló – turkey

    f. Sálúbàtà – sandal

    g. Ràkúnmí – camel

YORUBA BEADWORK

YORÙBÁ BEADWORK

h.   Pátá – panties

i.   Ọ̀bọ – monkey

j.   Màmá – mother

k.   Nanjú – relax

l.   Ehín – teeth

m.   Ìwé – book

n.   Jagunjagun – soldier

o.   Garawa – pail

p.   Fìlà – hat

q.   Eiye – bird

r.   Ajá – dog

s.   Ewé – leaf

t.   Koronfo – empty

http://www.hamillgallery.com/YORUBA/YorubaBeadwork/Beadwork/Bead...

Home Training and Greetings in the Yorùbá Culture

Yorùbá people are always proud of the home training to which they expose their children. Among these training is the tradition of "greeting." The Yorùbás do not allow their children to misbehave in any way. A child would be disciplined if he or she woke up in the morning and failed to greet the parents or the elderly person in the household.

Among Nigerians, Africans, and the World all over, the Yorùbás are very distinct in expressing utmost respect while greeting their parents and elderly persons. Other cultures may accept a child's hand shakes with their parents and elderly persons or just bend a little bit while greeting, but the Yorùbá boys have been trained to postrate or lie down flat on the floor, for example, while they say "good morning" to their parents and other elderly people. "Ẹ kàáró, or good morning mòmó/bàbá." Then the father or mother will respond and say "pèlé o Ògerò Omo olókùn ẹshin Kàáró, o ò jíire bí?" These are the child's "oríkis-the praise names." The boy will not change position until the parent or the elderly person has stopped. The same is applicable to a Yoruba girl. She must greet her parents in the morning; a boy lie down, while a girl kneel down and say, "e kàáró Bàbá mi." Then the parent will respond and say some of the oriki names of the girl, such as "pèlé o, Àsùnké, omo ẹkùn, ọmọ ọwá, sé ojí dada?" Then the girl will respond by saying, "a dúpé." Also, the girl must remain on her kneel, until her parents stopped the greeting.

Knowing how to greet, is part of growing up as a Yorùbá person, and the

YORÙBÁ IFÁ DIVINER'S BAG

YORÙBÁ, BEADED IFA BAG 12, Nigeria, 11", $300, © Tim Hamill

Used to carry divination objects and tools, the bags are worn in public ceremonies by Ifa priestesses and used and displayed in their homes. Beads were signs of wealth and status. The beaded front lifts up to reveal a pouch on the back panel.

http://www.hamillgallery.com/YORUBA/YorubaBeadwork/YorubaBags/Yor..

Yorùbá are so popular with this culture to the extent that they are labeled "ọmọ ẹ kàárọ̀ eè jíi re." Which simply means "the very greetful people? The Yorùbás also greet themselves when they want to sleep at night. This time you will hear them saying, Ó d' àa rò o, kí Ọlọ́run jí wa reo, which means "good night and may God wake us up in peace." Yorùbás also greet by saying "àlá ire o," meaning sweet dreams.

In Yorùbá land, there are special greetings for different times and occasions. Whether in an annual festival or in joyful or sad occasions. **ANSWER TO ALL THESE ARE "E SÉÉ ADÚPẸ́ O**; thank you, we are grateful.

YORÙBÁ BEADWORK

YORUBA, BEADED GUORD 15, Nigeria, 15", $400, © Tim Hamill

Beads were signs of wealth and status. Many Yorùbá sacred and secular objects were embellished with elaborate images and symbolic designs created by small glass beads.

The Tradition of Greeting in the Yoruba Land

Greetings	Response
<u>Greeting to welcome a friend:</u> Ękaabo, se daa daa lede (if you haven't seen the fellow for while, you say)	
	Adupę, ę se pupo/Fine, thank you
Eku ojo meta/It has been a while	Beeni oto ojo meta/Yes, it has been a while
Casual: Bawo ni?/What's up?	Daadaa ni, ese/Fine, thank you
Ękaaro/Good morning	Ękaaro/Good morning
Ekaa san/Good afternoon	Ękaasan/Good afternoon
Ękaa le/Good evening	Ękaale/Good evening
Eku irole/Good evening	Ęku irole/Good evening
<u>Greetings for good night:</u>	
O daaro/Good night	Odaaro/Good night
O dola/till tomorrow	O dola/till tomorrow
<u>Greetings for Farewell:</u>	
Odabo/bye bye	Odabo
A o pade layo/We'll meet again with joy	Amin/Amen
Ka fire pade/May we meet again in peace	Amin/Amen
Riri wa bii oyin/May our next meeting be as sweet as honey	Amin/Amen
<u>Greetings for good memory:</u>	
Ęku aigbagbe	Greeting for keeping up with it
Eku afi so kan	Greeting for keeping them in your mind
<u>Greetings for support:</u>	
Eku aajo ara yin	Thanks for caring
Eku aduro ti	Thanks for staying with me or for your support
Olorun ko ni ya wa	God will not let anything separate us
<u>Greeting People that are relaxing</u>	Answering
Plural-E ku faaji o–I greet you for relaxing O ku faaji o	Oo ęse, (Hey, thank you)

68

Ẹ kú inanra–I greet you for resting	Oo, ese, (Hey, thank you)	
Greeting people dancing:	Oo, ese, (Thank you)	
Ẹ kú ijo o		
Greeting an old person:		
Ẹ kú agba o		
Ojo alẹ dara – your evening times will be pleasant	Amin ẹ ṣe o (Amen, thank you)	
Greeting for Thanksgiving		
Eku ọdun idupẹ/ikoore–Happy Thanksgiving	Oo, ese o, emi wa o se amodun o. Amen, thank you	
Ẹ kú odun idupẹ/ikoore or Keresimesi–Christmas	May we all have many happy returns	
Greeting for Independence: Ẹ kú ewu odun ominira–Happy Independence Day	Oo, ese o, emi a samodun Thank you, may the next one come to pass in our sights	
Greeting someone who is sitting down: EKU'joko	Ekaabo/Welcome	
Eku isin–Greeting you for the worship	Oo, a o se ominran o Thank you, I'll see you in the worship next time	

Greetings for a Pregnant Woman:		Answering
1. Ẹ kú idura (or	I greet you for holding on	Ese, Adupẹ thank you very much
2. Isokale anfaani (or)	I wish you a peaceful delivery	
3. Afọn a gbo kóto so o (or)	May the delivery be peaceful	
4. Ao gbọ hun 'ya, ao gbo tomo o (or)	We will hear both voices, mother's and child	
5. Ti bi tire leo bi o (or)	I wish you all the best on the delivery	
6. Abiwere o	Your delivery day will be a pleasant surprise	

When a Pregnant Woman just had her baby:		Answering
1. Bárikà, ẹkú ewu ọmọ	Congratulations for the safe delivery	Amin
		Esé e, ire akárie
2. Omo titiun, O kú àtòrunbò	New baby welcome from heaven	Amen, thank you
3. Mo yọ fun yin ọmọ yọ funrà mi	I rejoice with you, I rejoice for myself	May blessings like this go round
4. Olúwà yoo dá ọmọ na si	The Lord will protect the child	
5. Olúwa yoo woo		
6. Omo yo lọwọ rere lẹhin	I pray the child will have brothers and sisters	
7. Yo se ọmọ kalé	The baby will be a good child	
8. Olúwa a somo ni bánkalé	The baby will not die young	
9. Orí ọmọ a gbó ẹsẹ a ranlẹò	The baby will grow to old	
10. Eku owo losun, eku owo lomi	I greet you for the intensive nursing	
Greetings for anybody that escaped accidents or danger:		Answering
1. Bárikà, ẹ kú orii re	Congratulations, you are so lucky	Amin o
2. E kú ewu	I greet you for the safe escape	Ẹ sẹe
3. Ẹ ku inú re	I greet you because your good virtue had come to your aid	Amen
		Thank you
4. Bó bá ku kolúwa yo ni o	May God continue to protect you	
5. Ẹ kú a kọyo	Greet you for the safety	
6. Ẹ kú a asalà	Greet you for surviving this	
7. A ò ni fi láburú o	Bad thing will not happen to us	
Greetings when someone lost his/her valuable properties like house, car, money, jewelry, etc.:		
1. Ẹ pèlé o	Sorry I sympathize with you	Ese o, ekú orò
2. Ẹ kú òfò	Sorry for the loss of your valuable	ènìyàn
3. Ekú àdánu		Thanks for caring
4. Ki Olúwa kó fi ofo rèmi	May the loss be a sacrifice for your life	
5. A kò ni ri irú èyi mó o	May this be the end of the misfortune	
6. Ọlọrun yoo fi mo bee o		Amen/Amin
7. Olórun yio fòp'o rópò	May God bless you abundantly.	Thanks/ esé púpò

Greetings when an old person dies:		Answering
1. Eku'dele momo/baba	Greetings for taking charge in the absence of mother/father	Esée, Eku-abase Thanks for coming
2. E ku asèyin de 3. E kú ìnáwó 4. Ehin babá/ehin iya a dára 5. Babaa yá (or) Iya á ya 6. Olórun yo basiri o	May his/her absence be mildly felt May God bless you	
Greetings for a new house:		Answering
1. E kú ináwo ilé yii	Greetings for spending on the house	Amen Thanks
2. Emi yio gbe Ilé yì, yió si turao	May you live to enjoy it	Esée, a dúpé
3. E ó ko eyi'tó - ju bee lo		
Greetings when you want to apologize:		Answering
Jowo ma binu si mi or	Please don't be mad with me	Odára/it's ok
E jowó e má binu si mi	Please don't be mad with me (for an elderly)	Odára/it's ok
O kú súuru	Thanks for your patience with me (or)	It's o.k. thank you
Eku suuru	Thanks for your tolerance	It's o.k./odára
Okú a fi ye dénú	Thanks for being patient	It's o.k./odára
Greetings for Sunday:		
Eku ojó isinmi	I greet you for Sunday	
E ku alaja ose	I greet you for getting through another week	Oo! A ó sò po re E sée, May we live to see many of them (Sunday)
Greeting for someone who is selling in the Market:		
Ekú ojà or o/kú ojà	Greet you for being in the market	O, e se. Thank you
Ekú oro aje	Greet you for the struggle to make money	

Greeting when you appreciate someone's intelligence:		
E kú àro jinle	Thanks for your deep thought	
E kú à foye gbé	Thanks for using your knowledge	Thank You E sée
E kú làa kàye	Thanks for the wisdom	Thank You/Ese
Dry Season Greeting:		
E kú eerùn yí	I greet you for this dry season	Oo eşé Thank you
E kú ogbelèyi	I greet you for the dryness	Oo ese/thank you
Ekú òòrùn yi	I greet you as it brightly sunny	oo jàre Thanks what shall we do?
Greeting while its raining:		
E kú òjò yi	I greet you for this rain	Oo eşé Thank you
E kú òginnintin yi	I greet you for the cool weather	Oo, ese
E kú òtútù yi	I greet you for coping with this cool weather	Oo, ese
Greeting when there is scarcity of food:		
E kú iyàn yí	I greet you for coping with scarcity	Oo, esé Thank you/May we be blessed
Ekú àhe je	I greet you for managing with what's left	Kín la tíse ǎ What shall we do
E kú owón onje yi		
Greeting when there is a surplusity of food:		
E kú opo ounjè yi	I greet you for this surplusity	Oo e sée Thank you
Ekú mundunmundun	I greet you for enjoying it all	
E kú amúje	I greet you for consuming it all	

72

Greeting for people that are fasting:		Answering
Ẹ kú òùngbẹ	I greet you for coping with thirst	À mín, o ẹse
Ẹ kú iṣẹ́ làadà	I greet you for denying yourself for divine course	Thank you
È mi o sáikà rè	May you live to see the end of the fasting period	Àmén/Àmín Thank you
Ẹmi o gbaaja	,,	,,
When a child or youth just died, we greet the deceased parents like this:		
Ẹ pẹ̀lẹ́ o	I am sorry	Ẹse o/thank you
Ẹ kú àmú mọ́ra	Greeting you for enduring the grief	Thank you/ese
Omi ló dànù Ọlọ́run	It could be worse	Thanks/ẹse o
Olúwa yó pèsè bámikalé	The Lord will provide the comforter with longevity	Thank you very much E see pup o
Olúwa yio pèsè omo elémìy gígùn	The Lord will provide another blessing	Amen/Àmín
Olúwa yo se dáada mìran	The Lord will transform this sadness into joy for you	Amen/Àmín eseé
Greeting when someone is having legal problems:		Answering
Ẹ kú wàhálà ejọ́ yi	I greet you for coping with this case	Ẹsée Thank you
Orí a dá e láre	Your head will see you through, God will justify you	Amen/Àmín Thank you/esee
Orí a kọ́ ẹ yo	Your head will see you through, God will justify you	Thank s/ẹ sẹ́ púpò
The Yoruba always give honor and respect they have to their kings and chiefs.		
This is how they greet the kings:		
Kábiyèsí	Your highness/your majesty	Ésé/thank you
Aláse èkejì òrìsà	The law maker like the gods	Esé/thank you

Kí adá pé Lórí	May your head keep the crow for long time	Amen/Àmín Thank you
Kíbàtà pé lésè	May your feet stay in the royal shoe for a long time	Amen/Àmín Thank you
E Ó je ju ará iwájú o	Long live the king, you will live longer than your descendants	„
This is how we greet our chief:	„	„
Ebo á fíń O	May the sacrifices be accepted	Àse/Amen/Àmín Thank you
Èru á dà	Your father will bless you and support you	Àse, eseé
E kú ètò ilú	Thanks for caring	Thank you/eseé

YORUBA BEADED CROWN

YORUBA, BEADED CROWN 2, Nigeria, 9", $500, SOLD, © Tim Hamill

Worn by the king, or Oba, in public ceremonies, they are embellished with symbolic designs. Beads were signs of wealth and status. The veil, here missing, seperated the divine king from mortals.

74

10 Many African peoples who do not produce figure sculpture carve and decorate their everyday objects most beautifully. This is a wooden stool, inlaid with copper and brass wire, used by elders among the AKamba. Manchester Museum. Diameter 9 in.

11 Similarly, the MaShona are best known for their decorative headrests, used like a pillow to protect their elaborate hair-styles. This one was collected at Umtali, Zimbabwe. Manchester Museum. Ht 4⅜ in.

12 Plastic art among the Lozi (formerly better known as the BaRotse) is best represented in museum collections by basketwork in their characteristic technique. They do, however, carve wooden bowls with animals on the lids. British Museum. L. 24½ in.

Àwọn Ọmọdé yĭ ńkî ìyá wọn.

These children are greeting their mother

Greetings in Yorùbá has no end and the responses to these greetings cannot be exhausted. The Yorubas are the most affectionate and most greetful people on the face of the earth.

Àtúnyèwò Ẹ̀kọ́ – Chapter Review/Exercise

1. Match each greeting expression in the first column with an appropriate greeting in the second column.

Greeting Expression

Time or Situation of the Greeting

1. Ẹ káàrò _____

    A. Greeting while in church

2. Ẹkáalẹ́ _____

    B. Welcome

3. Ẹkáàsón _____

    C. Greeting around 4-7 p.m.

4. Ẹkú ìsìn _____

    D. Greeting when you are sitting

5. Ẹ kú ìròlé _____

    E. Good morning

6. Ẹ káà bò _____

    F. Good afternoon

7. Bárìkà ekú ewu omo _____

    G. Good evening

8. Ẹ kú ìdúró _____

    H. When a new baby is born

9. Ẹ kú ìjòkó _____

    I. Greeting when you are standing

10. Ẹ kú ìdùra _____

    J. Fine thank you

11. Báwo ni nkan _____

    K. Greeting for pregnant woman

12. S'á làáfìa ni _____

    L. Good night

13. Ódàarò _____

    M. Fine thank you

Useful Everyday Conversation

Conversation with a friend	Response
Ekáàbọ o/Welcome	Ẹkú ilé/Hi
S'álàfià ni/How are you?	Adúpẹ́/Fine thank you
Kín ni Orúkọ yín	Orúkọ mi ni Dr. Scoth/My name is Dr. Scoth
	Ọmọ Ìlú Atlanta Georgia USA
Níbo ni Ìlú yin/Where are you from?	Ìlú mi ni Atlanta Georgia, USA
Ọmọ yín ńkó/How is your child?	Ó wà dada/he/she is fine
Bàbá ńkọ́/How is your dad?	Wọ́n wà dada/he is fine
Níbo lẹ̀n lọ/Where are you going?	Mò ńlọ si'ojà/I am going to the market
Kín lẹ̀ ńlọ rà/What are you going to buy?	Mo fẹ́ lọ rá oúnje/I am going to buy groceries.
Níbo ni ojà wâ/Where is the market located?	Ojà wâ níwájú Ààfin/The market is facing the palace.
Báwo lòja ṣe jìnà sí/How far is the market?	Ibùsọ̀ Kan ni ojà síbí/The market is not more than one mile from here.
Ódàbọ̀, ẹmá pẹ́o/O.K., bye bye, don't be long.	Ódàbọ̀/bye.

How to Receive a Company at Home

Action	Responses
Ta lókan'lẹ̀kùn/Who is knocking or who is it?	Èmi ni ò/It is me
Ìwọ tani ò/Who are you?	Èmi Láyíwọlá ni o/It is me Láyíwọlá.
Ah, bùròdá 'Láyí ekáàbọ̀!/Ah brother 'Láyí Welcome!	Ẹkú'le ó! Gbogbo ènìyàn/Hi everybody! (If everybody is present)
Sẹ́ dáadáa ledé/How are you?	Adúpẹ́ dúpẹ́, esẹ́/Fine thank you.
Bàbá àti Mọmọ́ nko? How is Mom and dad	Wọ́n wa dada They are fine thank you.
Óyá ẹjẹ́ká lọ Let's go	Ó ti yá/ I am ready
Sẹ́ ẹ mú owó lọ́wọ́ Hope you take money with you	Bẹ́ẹni/Yes mo mú owó lọ́wọ́
Èló ni eja/How much is the fish?	Ogún Náírà in idìkan/20.00 per pack
Èló ni iṣu/How much is the yam?	Ogbọ̀n Náírà ni ò kòọ̀ kan, it is 30.00 each
Èló ni aṣo/How much is the cloth?	Náírà mẹ́wǎ ni ọpá kan, it is 10.00 per yard
Èló ni mo jẹ yiń/How much do I owe you?	Náírà méjìlá pérẹ́ ni eje mí

Yes = Bẹ́ẹni
No = Óti/rárá or bẹ́ẹkọ́

Yoruba numbers assume different forms, of counting, (1) the cardinal, (2) adverbial (or) time counting, (3) ordinal counting, (4) total counting, (5) counting in thousands, and (6) distributive counting. The following list exhibits the Yorùbá cardinal numerals and their constructions:

Construction of Cardinals

The cardinal units, from <u>two</u> to <u>ten</u> have "m" prefixed to them when they belong to nouns expressed or understood, as eniyan mewa, ten people. Méní or Ení, is used only in counting (i.e) Cardinal (a) as follows:

1.	ókan	16.	eríndínlógún (20-4)
2.	éjì	17.	ẹtádínlógún (20-3)
3.	ẹ́ta	18.	ejídínlógún (20-2)
4.	ẹrin	19.	okándínlógún (20-1)
5.	arûn	20.	ogún
6.	efà	21.	okánlèlógún (20+1)
7.	éje	22.	ejílèlógún (20+2)
8.	ẹ́jo	23.	ẹtálèlógún (20+3)
9.	ẹ́san	24.	erínlèlógún (20+4)
10.	ẹwá	25.	édógbòn (30-5)
11.	okánla	26.	mérìndínlógbòn (30-4)
12.	ejìlá	27.	mẹ́ta dínlógbòn (30-3)
13.	erinla	28.	méjìnlógbòn (30-2)
14.	erìnlá	29.	mókàndínlógbòn (30-1)
15.	ẹdógún	30.	ogbòn

80

Contemporary Female Hairstyle in the Irun Kíkó Style.

This variation is called "Eko Bridge" and its curvilinear network is
intended to recall the bridges in Lagos.

Let's count from 1 - 100 in cardinal form. Eje kaka lati ookan de ogorun ni cardinal.

1. ókan
2. méjì
3. méta
4. mérin
5. marún
6. méfà
7. méje
8. méjo
9. mésàn
10. méwà
11. mókànlá
12. méjìlá
13. métàlá
14. mérìnlá
15. medógún
16. mérìndínlógún
17. métàdínlógún
18. méjìdínlógún
19. mókàndínlógún
20. ogún
21. mókànlélógún
22. méjìlélógún
23. métàlélógún
24. mérìnlélógún
25. marúndínlógbòn
26. mérìndínlógbòn
27. métàdínlógbòn
28. méjìdínlógbòn
29. mókàndínlógbòn
30. ogbòn
31. mokànlélógbòn
32. méjìlélógbòn
33. métàlélógbòn
34. mérìnlélógbòn
35. marúnlélógbòn
36. mérìndínlógójì
37. métàdínlógójì
38. méjìdínlógójì
39. mókàndínlógójì
40. ogójì
41. mókànlélógójì
42. méjìlélógójì
43. métàlélógójì
44. mérìnlélógójì
45. marúnlélógójì
46. mérindínláàdóta
47. métàdínláàdóta
48. mejìdínláàdóta
49. mokàndínláàdóta
50. àdóta
51. mókànléláàdóta
52. méjìléláàdóta
53. metàlelaadota
54. mérìnléláàdóta
55. marúnléláàdóta
56. merìndínlógóta
57. métadínlógóta
58. méjìndínlógóta
59. mókàndínlógóta
60. ogóta
61. mókànlélógóta
62. mejìlélógóta
63. métàlélógóta
64. mérìnlélógóta
65. marúnlélógóta
66. mérìndínláàdórin
67. métàdínláàdórin
68. méjìdínláàdórin
69. mókàndínláàdórin
70. àdórin
71. mókàndínláàdórin
72. méjìléláàdórin
73. metàléláàdórin
74. mérìnléláàdórin
75. marúnléláàdórin
76. mérindínlógórin
77. métadínlógórin
78. méjìdínlógórin
79. mókàndínlógórin
80. ogórin
81. mokànlélógórin
82. méjìlélógórin
83. metàlélógórin
84. mérìnlélógórin
85. marúnlélógórin
86. mérìndínláàdórún
87. métàdínláàdórún
88. méjìdínláàdórún
89. mókàndínláàdórun
90. àadórún
91. ookànléláàdórún
92. méjìléláàdórún
93. métàléláàdórún
94. mérìnléláàdórún
95. marúnléláàdórún
96. mérìndínlógórún
97. métadínlógórún
98. méjìdínlógórún
99. mókàndínlógórún
100. ogórún

Exercise:*

1. Try and write by 'heart' numbers 1 to 50 in Yoruba cardinals. (a)

2. Write from 51-100 in Yoruba cardinal form.(b)

3. Dollar mewa pere ni iwe je/the book cost only $10.00.

Now construct ten sentences as above.

4. Elo ni bata? How much is the show?

Now construct ten sentences as above using alphabet pictures for name of objects.

82

Gèlèdé Headdress with Panumo Hairstyle
Yorùbá, Nigeria
Wood

Collection of the National Museum, Lagos, Nigeria.
Photo by Frank Speed, 1971.

ADVERBIAL OR TIME COUNTING

In numeral adverbs, the cardinal adverbs, signifying the number of times an event takes place. They are formed by prefixing "L" (li, as in) "e̩" a contraction of "e̩rin" or "le̩merin" (four times). See more below:

Once – le̩kan

Twice – léèmejì

Thrice – léèmé̩ta

Four times – léè̩mé̩rin

Five times – lèemarǔn

Six times – lé̩è̩mé̩fà

Seven times – lé̩è̩meje

Eight times – lé̩è̩me̩jo̩

Nine times – lé̩è̩mé̩sǎn

Ten times – léè̩mé̩wǎ

20 times – ló̩nà ogún

30 times – ló̩nà ogbò̩n

40 times – ló̩nà ogó̩jì

50 times – ló̩nà áádó̩ta

60 times – ló̩nà o̩gó̩ta

70 times – ló̩nà áádó̩rin

80 times – ló̩nà ogó̩rin

90 times – lò̩nà áádó̩rǔn

233 *Ibeji*, single figures of twins. On the left is the example carved by Lamidi, with copies by his apprentices Joseph Fakeye, Amusa Akande and Ganiyu Fakeye. Coll. F. Willett. Hts $12\frac{3}{4}$, $11\frac{7}{8}$, $11\frac{3}{8}$, $11\frac{1}{8}$in.

100 times – lọ́nà ọgọ́rùn

200 times – lọ́nà igba

300 times – lọ́nà ọdúnrún

400 times – lọ́nà irinwó (àti bẹ́ẹ̀ bẹ́ẹ̀ lọ) (etc.)

Exercise: (i.e.) Mo Pe Adé Lẹ́ẹkan/I called Ade Once. Now construct then sentences

following the example above.

COUNTING IN ORDINAL

The ordinals from one to nineteen are formed by prefixing "ek" the choice

being determined by the law of euphonic concord) to the cardinal as shown below.

1st – èèkínní

2nd – èèkejì

3rd – ẹ̀ẹ̀kẹta

4th – èèkerin

5th – ẹẹkarùn

6th – ẹ̀ẹkéfà

7th – èèkeje

8th – ẹ̀ẹ̀kejọ

9th – èèkesàn

10th – ẹ̀ẹkewá

Exercise: Example will be constructed without elision and with elision, i.e., Bade gba ipo'kinni (with elision) (Bade gba ipọ ekinni/Bade came first in the class). (Bunmi gba ipo eekeji/Bunmi gba ipo'keji Bunmi came 2nd.) Now construct five sentences following the examples above both without elision and with elision on a "T" table.

59 Tray used in Ifa divination collected at Ardra (Allada) in Bénin (Dahomey) during the first half of the seventeenth century. Yoruba. Weickmann Collection, Ulm Museum. 22 × 13¾ in.

56 A modern board for Ifa divination from Bénin (Dahomey). The colours and motifs should be compared with *Ill. 23*. The face at the top is said by Bascom to represent Eshu, the principle of uncertainty in the Yoruba pantheon. Linden Museum, Stuttgart. 9 × 7½ in.

TOTAL COUNTING

Both two – méjéèjì (i.e.) Fun mi ni eja mejeeji

Both two – mééjèèjì

Both three – métèèta

Both four – mérèèrin

Both five – máráàrún

Both six – méféèfà

Both seven – méjèèje

Both eight – méejèèjo

Both nine – mésèèsán

All ten – méwèèwá

Example: Funmi ní eja merèèin/Let me have the four fish. (Now construct five sentences of your own). (See alphabet pictures for name of objects).

COUNTING IN THOUSAND

1,000 – egbèrún kan
(200 x 5)

2,000 – egbèrún méjì/egbàa
(200 x 10)

3,000 – egbèrún méta/égbeédógùn
(200 x 15)

4,000 – egbèrún mérin/ègbàajì
(2000 x 2)

5,000 – egbèrún márùn/egbèédógbòn
(200 x 25)

6,000 – egbèta
(2000 x 3)

Awọn ọkunrin meji yi nta ayo.

POPULAR YORÙBÁ GAME

7,000 ẹ̀dégbaàrin 8000 – 1000

8,000 – ẹgbàarin
(2000 x 4)

9,000 – ẹ̌dégbaàrun
(10,000-1000)

10,000 – ẹgbàarún
(2000 x 5)

12,000 - ẹgbàafà
(2000 x 6)

14,000 – ẹgbàaje
(2000 x 7)

16,000 – ẹgbàajó
(2000 x 8)

18,000 – ẹgbàasǎn
(2000 x 9)

20,000 – ẹgbàwá
(2000 x 10) or oke' kan (one bag)

100,000 – ọ̀ké márǔn (5 bags)

1,000,000 – àadóta ọ̀ké (50 bags)

2,000,000 – ogórǔn ọ̀ké (100 bags)

Example: egbèrún mẹ́ta ènìyàn ló wá si'sósì lánǎn 3,000 people showed up at the church yesterday. (Construct your own five sentences as above).

DISTRIBUTIVE NUMERALS

Distributive of numbers or quantity, formed as follows: by doubling the cardinals that commence with "m" as:

One each – ọ̀kòòkan

Oríkì Òrúnmìlà - Praising the Spirit of Divination

Òrúnmìlà, Èlérí Ìpín
  Òrúnmìlà, witness of fate
Ibìkejì Olódùmarè
  Second to the Olódùmarè (god)
Àjéjù Oògùn
  Thou art far more efficacious then medicine.
Òbìrìtì, Apijó Ikú Dà
  Thou the Immense orbit, that averts the day of death.
Olúwa Mì Ató Ibá J'ayé
  My Lord, Almighty to save,
Orò, Abikú J'ìgbo
  Mysterious Spirit that fought death, to thee salutation is first due in the n
Ògègé Agbáiyé Gún
  Thou Equilibrium that adjusts world forces.
Òdùdù Tì'Ndú Ori'Emèrè
  Thou art the one whose exertion it is to reconstruct the creatures of bad l
Tún Ori'Tì Kò Sun Wòn Se A
  Repairer of ill-luck.
Amò Ìkú
  He who knows thee becomes immortal
Olówa Àíyéré
  Lord, the Indesposable King.
Àgíri Ile'Ilogbón
  Perfect in the house of Wisdom.
Olúwà Mi Àmòìmòtán
  My Lord, Infinite in knowledge.
A Kò Mò Ò Tán Kò Se
  For not knowing thee in full, we are futile.
Àbá Mò Ó Tán Ìbá Sè Ké
  Oh, if we could but know thee in full, all will be well with us.

Two each – méjì-méjì

Three each – méta-méta

Four each – mérin-mérin

Five each – márùn-márùn

Six each – méfà-méfà

Seven each – méje-méje

Eight each – méjo-méjo

Nine each – mésàn-mésàn

Exercise: (i.e.) Ayò àti Fúnmi pín ẹyin mẹ́wà nâ ni márùn márùn/Ayò and Fúnmi divided the ten eggs five each. Now construct your own sentences following example above. You may check the picture alphabet for possible na,es of objects.

EXERCISE 1

Write the following numbers in Yorùbá Numerals, Ko àwon númbà yi ni Yorùbá.

1. 43 –

2. 10 –

3. 80 –

4. 06 –

5. 56 –

6. 100 –

7. 16 –

8. 90 –

9. 10 –

10. 02 –

YORUBA STOOL

Photographs © Tim Hamill

YORUBA, STOOL 1, 19", $400, Nigeria

Yoruba stools, like those of the Luba, related to kings and important chiefs, who defined their power by the display of prestige objects during important ceremonies. Stools were among the most important of these objects. The leader was literally as well as figuratively supported by a male or female caryatid figure, which also symbolizes the continuity of power.

11. 70 –

12. 09 –

EXERCISE 2

Ko nɔ́mbà wɔnyí lɔ́rɔ̀ – Write these numbers in Yorùbá words.

1. 3 _____

2. 6 _____

3. 20 _____

4. 18 _____

5. 12 _____

6. 01 _____

7. 22 _____

8. 42 _____

9. 31 _____

10. 40 _____

11. 55 _____

12. 57 _____

13. 62 _____

14. 27 _____

15. 99 _____

16. 100 _____

17. 82 _____

18. 77 _____

37 Terracotta head from a figure found during tin-mining at Nok, northern Nigeria. The eyes are represented in characteristic Nok style. The rings representing the hair, the pendent locks, and the hair-band are paralleled in the later sculptures from Ife. Jos Museum. Ht 8¼ in.

19. 38 _____

20. 35 _____

EXERCISE 3

Write the answers of the following in both Yorùbá and English numerals. Example:
ookan ati ookan 1+1 = eeji 2

1. ẹẹ́ta àti oókan = _____

2. ẹẹta àti eéjì = _____

3. ẹẹ́fà ati oókan = _____

4. ẹẹrin àti oókan = _____

5. ẹẹ́jo àti èeji = _____

6. ẹẹ́fà àti eéjì = _____

7. eéjì àti ẹẹ́jo = _____

8. aárǔn àti eéfà = _____

9. eésǎn àti eéjì = _____

10. eéjì àti oókan = _____

EXERCISE 4

ÌSIRÒ – MORE ADDITION

Write the answers in Yorùbá words only.

1. 10+10+10+7 = _____

2. 10+10+10+3 = _____

3. 10+10+10+3 = _____

4. 10+10+10+5 = _____

231 Pair of doors carved about 1910 by Olowe for
the Palace of the Ogoga of Ikere, showing Captain
Ambrose in a litter with his retinue being received
by the Ogoga wearing his beaded crown and
flanked by his attendants and wives. The degree to
which Olowe's figures are carved free of the
background is indicated by the broken figure at the
bottom right. British Museum. Ht approx. 6 ft.

5.   70+1+2+4 = _____

6.   80+5+6+5 = _____

7.   9+2+5+8 = _____

8.   20+2+40 = _____

9.   40+20+10 = _____

10.   10+5+7+2 = _____

EXERCISE 5

Write these numbers in Yorùbá words.

1.   20 _____

2.   15 _____

3.   25 _____

4.   28 _____

5.   40 _____

6.   41 _____

7.   11 _____

8.   13 _____

9.   88 _____

10.   44 _____

EXERCISE 6

Write the answers to the following in English numerals.

1.   eéjì _____

2.   eésàn _____

176, 177, 178 Each medium may have its own style. Azande wood sculptures are much more stylized than their pottery sculpture. The two figures are thought to represent ancestors and to have been used in the rituals of the *Mani* Society. British Museum. Hts 31½, 20¾ and 13 in.

3. oókànlá _____

4. ẹẹ́tàdínlógún _____

5. ogóji̖ _____

6. ogóta _____

7. àádórin _____

8. éjọ _____

9. àárùn _____

10. eérìndínlógóji̖ _____

11. ogbọ̀n _____

12. ẹẹ́fà̖ _____

13. ogórin _____

14. eérìndínlógóta _____

15. eéwà̖ _____

16. ogórŭn _____

17. àádórŭn _____

18. oókànlégóta _____

19. eéjìléláàdọ́rin _____

20. àádorín _____

EXERCISE 7

1. Define the following types of counting below with five examples for each.
   a. Cardinal counting

100

YORÙBÁ, GÈLÈDÉ MASK #18, 11", Nigeria $600 SOLD

Gèlèdé, a male association, uses the aesthetic power of sculpture, costume, song and dance to placate and please women, who have special spiritual power. Often with elaborate superstructures, the headdresses appear as identical pairs in the dances. To complete the show we have hung some Yorùbá beaded sashes, bags and vests with depicted heads.

b.   Ordinal counting

c.   Adverbial counting/Time Counting

d.   Distributive counting

e.   Counting in thousands

f.   Total Counting

2.   Differentiate between Adverbial Counting and Cardinal Counting with "5" examples of each number.

3.   List five examples of distributive counting and illustrate their daily application.

4.   Write the following Yorùbá words in <u>number</u> and state the <u>type of counting</u> they belong to:

a.   méjo

b.   léèmerin

c.   Léèmésàn

d.   Èèkefà

e.   Èèkéwà

f.   Èèkeje

g.   Métèeta

h.   Mérèèrin

i.   Méjèejo

j.   Egbèrún méta

k.   Egbèrún mésàn

Yorùbá (Yorba, Yorouba), Benin, Nigeria and Togo

***Olumeye* female figure.** The Yorùbá people, numbering over 12 million, are the largest nation in Africa with an art-producing tradition. Most of them live in southwest Nigeria, with considerable communities further west in the Republic of Benin and in Togo, in an area of forest and savannah. *Olúmèye* means "one who knows honor" and some Yorùbá carvers referred to the kneeling female figure as "a messenger of the spirit" who carries cola and cakes in a bowl. Carvings of this type were used in the reception room of the palace to hold kola nuts, which were given to the guests as an act of hospitality and for their refreshment.

Material: wood

Size: H. 37", W. 10", D. 9"

Price: $365   [#B110]

l. Méjì méjì

m. Méjọ méjọ

n. Mẹ́wà mẹwǎ

o. Méje mẹ́je

p. Ogójì ogójì

q. Ádọ́ta dọ́ta

r. Lọ́nà ọgọ́ta

s. Lọ́nà aadọ́rin

t. Èkarún

It is no secret that the Yoruba had the "first" of just about everything in
Nigeria and probably Africa. The first television station, the first institution of higher
learning (along with a first-rate teaching hospital), the first truly viable economy of
Nigeria and Africa with a sophisticated structure of business, investments and
banking institutions (remember the Industrial Investment Credit Corporation or
I.I.C.C.); the list goes on. The first winner of any Nobel Prize was a Nigerian of
Yoruba nationality, Wolé Sóyínká. In addition, if one takes a look at reputable
International Organizations such as the World Health Organization and the United
Nations among others, Yorùbá occupy positions requiring high levels of political and
technical sophistication. Because, the Yorùbá, more than any other group in Nigeria
have always embraced education, even though they may at the same time be involved
in business ventures. Education, amongst the Yorùbá, is what gives you honor and
respect among peers and family (Awósìkà, 1997).

Yorùbá culture and expressions were not written (using a set of alphabets)
until the 16th century, even though signs were used to convey messages way before
then. Before the invention of alphabet, education was largely restricted to the rich
and members of royalty. Texts of information were often carved into wooden tablets,
making them rather expensive to own. After the introduction of letters, the quest for
education among the middle class and the poor grew dramatically (Education, 2001).

Since Yoruba were mostly farmers, agricultural sciences took precedence in education but other subjects like history, mathematics and biological scineces were also taught. Many traveled far and wide to FreeTown, Timbuktu, Mali (the location of the first school of higher education in the world) to seek higher learning. Now, there are about 25 public and private universities located in Yorùbá regions of Nigeria alone. The Ọbéfémi Awolowo University at Ile Ife, which is twice the size of the University of Texas at Austin, conducts a bulk of Nigerian research (Education, 2001).

Through the traditional educational institution, the Yorùbá pass on the most cherishable values of the nation to its young. Education here is not conceived as an isolated institution; it is pervasived and embedded in the other cultural institutions. The cultural milieu of the child is the proper locus for his/her education. Traditional education emphasizes good conduct and character; it is the training of a complete human person, referred to as "omoluabi". This is the epitome of character (ìwà). Ìwà is the highest moral quality expected of any human person. For it is its possession that ensures good moral conduct. The Yorùbá people do not appreciate wealth which is not accompanied by charter. A child is trained to respect elders, to be honest, to be hardworking, generous, courageous and helpful to the needy. Hard work is especially emphasized and many children learn the classic Yorùbá rhyme on hard work from the cradle. (National, May 31-June 2002)

In traditional education, the community itself is the teacher and the school, and education is a life-time process, starting with the fetus until death. In pregnancy, the mother to be has guidelines about what to do, eat and drink for the sake of the child. Moreover, the devination system provides for a foreknowledge of the destiny of the fetus so as to prepare adequately for its birth and upbringing. At birth, the new baby is showered with love and affection by the entire extended family and community. As explained under naming ceremonies, the baby is given names according to the tradition of his/her household. As the baby grown, she is reminded of the meaning of her name, and then given instructions on how to live according to its meaning. The mother has this responsibility, and she performs it with pride. She recites the praise names of the child's family and the self-esteem of the child is thus enhanced from birth (National, May 31-June 2002).

As the child grows, informal training in numbering and language begin to take shape. At this point, the responsibility lies with grown-ups in the compound. He goes out to the playground with them, as he goes to the farm with them. They tell him trickster tales, and team teach him how to play the ayo game. Through the examples of elders, the child learns the virtues of endurance, courage, and through proverbs he learns the use of language and the art of living. The child is soon ready to learn a trade or craft. It may be a craft that is unique to the family (sculpture) or one that he has to go out and learn (tailoring). The parents are responsible for guiding the child and sending him/her to an apprentice and for getting him or her started in the new trade after graduation. In short, the focus of traditional Yoruba education is making the child a whole person and integral members of the community (National, May 31-June 2002).

Western education came into Yorùbá land in the early 19th century through the effort of Christian missionaries. Bishop Samuel Àjàyi Crowther, the first African Bishop was the first Yorùbá to receive higher education. History was made in 1952 when Chief Ọbáfẹ́mi Awólówọ̀ led the action group to election victory in the Western House of Assembly that his government was going to give priority to education and health within the limits of its budget. In his speech, Chief Awólówọ̀ declared: "Educational development is imperative and urgent. It must be treated as a national emergency, second only to war. It must move with the momentum of a revolution." (Western Region Debates, 30 July 1952, pp. 463-70 cited in fanfunwa, History of Education in Nigeria, p. 168).

This initiative was pursued with vigor. The government embarked on an elaborate campaign to win the hearts of the people to the idea of universal primal education. And it worked. Enrollment in primary school in the region jumped from 457,000 pupils in 1954 to 811,000 in 1955. By 1958, more than one million children were enrolled in primary schools in the region. This also had a positive effect on secondary school and teacher training expansion. In addition, trade schools and technical colleges were introduced throughout the region, and the region became a model for other regions in Nigeria. This initial effort of the Action Group let government in Western Region is responsible for the educational advancement of the Yoruba. This is why they consider it an outrage when Dr. Jubril Aminu of the Nigerian Universities Commission started a campaign to slow down educational achievements of the Southern parts of the country for the North to catch up, this achievement was not earned at the expense of any part of the country. It was achieved through foresight and sacrifice. As Funfunwa puts it, with the Universal Primary Education in Western region in 1955, "the boldest and perhaps the most unprecedented scheme in Africa south of the Sahara was launched by an indigenous government as a meaningful demonstration of its commitment to the vital interests of the people it governed." (p. 168). This revolution continued with the establishment of the University of Ife in 1962.

The Federal Republic of Nigeria is located on the West Coast of Africa with 36 states and recorded population of over 120 million people. Of this population, 30 million are students. The country is rich in petroleum and many other natural resources. The three dominant tribes are Yoruba in the southwest, Ibo in the eastern region and Hausa in the north. Although people speak their native languages, however the official language is English. The dominant two religions are Christianity and Islam. Nigeria gained it's independence from the British in 1960. For 15 years, it was under military rule. During this period, the tertiary institutions were plagued with riots and strikes resulting in a decline in quality of the education system. Educational institutions are still in the process of recuperating from the neglect of the former governments. A democratic government was voted for in February 1999. Retired General Olúsẹ́gun Ọbásanjọ́ was elected president. The Federal Government of Nigeria regards educations as an instrument for effecting national development. Her philosophy on education is based on the development of the individual into a sound and effective citizen and the provision of equal education opportunities for all citizens of the nation at the primary, secondary and tertiary levels both inside and outside the formal school system. The language of instruction in Nigerian institutions is English. The Federal Ministry of Education is the government body charged with the duty of regulating procedures and maintaining standards (Fáfúnwá, 1994).

Primary education begins at the age of six for the majority of Nigerians. Students spend six years in primary school and graduate with a school-leaving certificate. Subjects taught at the primary level include mathematics, English language, Bible knowledge, science and one of three main native languages (Hausa, Yorùbá and Ibo). Private schools would also offer computer science, French and art. Primary school students are required to take a Common Entrance Examination to qualify for admission into the Federal and State Government schools. Students spend six years in Secondary School. At the end of three years, they take the Junior Secondary School exam (JSS3 exam) that is a qualifying exam for Senior Secondary School. By Senior Secondary School Class 2 (SS2), students are taking the GCE O'level's exam, that is not mandatory, but most students take it to prepare for the Senior Secondary School Exam. The Senior Secondary School Exam is taken in the last year of high school (SS3). Private organizations, the State government or the Federal government manages secondary schools in Nigeria (Fáfúnwá, 1974).

With the introduction of 6-3-3-4 system of education in Nigeria, students are required to enter secondary school after spending a minimum of six years of Primary Education and passed a prescribed National Common Entrance Examination. The students must spend a minimum period of six years in Secondary School. During

110

this period, students are expected to spend three years in Junior Secondary School. The General Certificate of Education (GCE) was replaced by the Senior Secondary Certificate Examination (SSCE). The SSCE is conducted at the end of the Secondary School studies in May/June. The GCE is conducted in October/November as a supplement for those students who did not get the required credits from their SSCE results. The standards of the two examinations are basically the same. A body called West African Examination Council (WAEC) conducts both the SSCE and GCE. A maximum of nine and a minimum of seven subjects are registered for the examination by each student with Mathematics and English language taking as compulsory.

A maximum of nine grades are assigned to each subject ranging from: A1, A2, A3 or A1, B2, B3, B4 (Equivalent to Distinctions Grade) C4, C5, C6 or B4, B5, B6, (Equivalent to Distinctions Grade) C4, C5, C6, or B4, B5, B6, (Equivalent to Credit Grade), P7, P8, or D7, D8, or E (Just Pass Grade), F9, (Fail Grade).

Credit grades and above is considered academically adequate for entry into any University in Nigeria. In some study programs, many of the universities may require grades to get admission. The Federal Government policy on education is adhered to by all secondary schools in Nigeria. Six years of elementary school is followed by six years of secondary school, divided into the Junior Secondary and Senior Secondary School. Junior Secondary School consists of the JSSI, JSS2, and JSS3 that is equivalent to the 7th, 8th and 9th Grade respective. The Junior Secondary Certificate Examination (JSCE) is taken at the end of the junior year. Students who pass the exam may proceed to senior school at the same institution or may transfer to an institution of their choice. Senior Secondary School consists of the SSI, SS2 and SS3 that is equivalent to the 10th, 11th and 12th Grade. The Senior Secondary School Examination (SSCE) is taken at the end of the SS3. The West African Examination Council (WAEC) administers both exams. Three to six months after a student has taken the SSCE examination, they are issued an official transcript from their institution. This transcript is valid for one year, after which an official transcript from the West African Examination Council is issued (Fanfunwa, 1994).

All Senior Secondary students are required to study English, Mathematics, one science subject and one Nigerian language. All the other subjects are electives and are selected based on the students' interest be in the Sciences, Social Sciences or the Arts. The Senior Secondary Certificate Examination is one of the requirements for undergraduate admission into Nigerian University. A student must get at least a C in english and four other courses relevant to his major. A student applying for admission to study Medicine, Computer Science or Accounting, for example, will be required to have a minimum of a C in mathematics as well as in English. The second requirement is the Universities Matriculation Examination (UME) that was first conducted in 1978 by the Joint Admissions and Matriculation Board (JAMB). Decree No. 2 of 1978 (amended by Decree No. 3 or 1989) empowers the JAMB to conduct Matriculation Examinations for entry into all degree awarding institutions in Nigeria and place suitably qualified candidates in the available spaces in the institutions. Students may register for English language and any three subjects based on their particular major. A fifty-percent total score is considered a pass for the UME exam. However, different institutions have different minimum requirements based on the different majors. The language of instruction in Nigerian institutions is English. Students who have graduated from the secondary schools with a credit in English language often meet the required minimum of 173 points on the TOEFL (Fanfunwa, 1994).

The government has majority control of university education. The Federal Government of Nigeria had adopted education as an instrument for national development. Nigeria's philosophy of education is based on the integration of the individual into a sound and effective citizenry. There is to be equal edicational opportunities for all citizens of the nation at the primary, secondary and tertiary levels. In addition to the number of universities, there are 13 Federal and 14 State owned Polytechnic Colleges respectively. These were established to train technical, middle-level manpower. Some of the colleges are beginning to award degrees. English language is the medium of instruction. The Academic Year is from October to September. Entry Requirements include: miminum of SSCE/GCE Ordinary Level Credits at maximum of two sittings. Minimum cut-off marks in Joint Admission and Matriculation Board Entrance Examination (JAMB) of 200 and above out of a maximum of 400 marks are required. Candidates with minimum of Merit Pass in National Certificates minimum qualifications with minimum of 5 O/L Credits given direct entry admission into the appropriate undergraduate degree programs. Duration of undergraduate programs in Nigerian Universities depends largely on the program

113

of study (Fafunwa, 1974).

Nigeria Universities are generally grouped. Five of these universities were established between 1948 and 1965, following the recommendation of Ashby Commission set up by the British Colonial Government to study the needs for University education for Nigeria. These Universities are fully funded by the Federal Government. They were established primarily to meet the manpower needs of Nigeria and set basic standards for University Education in the country. These universities have continued to play their roles for manpower developments and their provisions of standards, which have helped to guide the subsequent establishments of other generations and States Universities in Nigeria. With the increasing population of qualified students for University education in Nigeria and the growing needs for scientific and technological developments, setting up more Universities became imperative. Between 1970 and 1985, 12 additional Universities were established and located in various parts of the country. The need to establish Universities to address special areas of Technological and Agricultural demand prompted the setting up of ten additional universities between 1985 and 1999. Pressures from qualified students from each state who could not readily get admissions to any of the Federal Universities continue to mount on States Governments. It became imperative and urgent for some State Governments to invest in the establishments of Universities. In recognition of the need to encourage private participation in the provision of university education, the Federal Government established a law in 1993, allowing private sectors to establish universities following guidelines prescribed by the Government (Fafunwa, 1994).

Exercise

1. Compare and contrast the Nigeria Education System with American Education System (i.e.) from K-12.

2. Describe the term West African Examination Council and briefly state its importance to a high school Yoruba student.

3. What is the importance of JAMB (that is Joint Admission and Matriculation Board Entrance Examination).

4. Describe the relationship of the Federal government with the Nigerian Universities.

5. What subjects do all senior secondary students are required to study.

6. Explain these terms.
    a. SSCE
    b. SS2
    c. GCEO Level
    d. G-3-3-4 System of Education

7. Briefly explain the influence of Chief Ọbáfẹ́mi Awólọ́wọ̀ in Nigeria Education.

8. Explain briefly the importance of education to the Yorùbá people.

9. How did Western education penetrate into the Yorùbá land?

10. What grades are considered academically adequate for entry into any University in Nigeria?

In the past, there were many ways by which people guessed the time of the day. Sunrise and sunset, the exact position of the sun in the sky can almost provide an accurate time of the day.

Shadow is another way by which time can be reckoned. Shadow would be measured with the time of day. However, time clocks and watches have been invented to replace the old ways of time reckoning.

Ni igbà iwásẹ́, orísirísi ọ̀nàn ni afi rímo àkókò ojó. À nlo yíyo òrùn, bẹ̀ni asi nlo ipò ti òòrùn wa ni sánmọ̀ àti ojiiji se òdiwọ̀n àkókò. Sùgbón ni aiyé òdé òni, aago ọwọ́ àti aago tábìlì tiwa ti anlo lati mọ kínni agogo wi. Other examples: Àsìkò (idákọmu/8-9 am) (ni òrùn yọ/7 am) (ni òòrùn wọ̀/6 pm) (ìròlé/4 pm) (ni fẹ̀rẹ̀mójú/5-6 am) (ni ìdáji/1-4 am) (ààjìn/12 am) (ni ìdasán/12 pm) (ìyáléta/9-11:50)

EXERCISE 1

Draw and show the correct time as written below. Use the cardinal forms of Yorùbá numeral. On each diagram, write "kínni agogo wi? that is what time it is? (*"kojá" = past, kù = before, ààbọ̀ = 30 minutes or half of the hour).

1.   Agogo mẹ́wà kojá isẹ́jú márùn – The time is 5 minutes past 10.

2.   Agogo méjì kojá isẹ́jú méjì –

3.   Agogo mẹ́rin kojá isẹju mẹ́wà –

4.   Agogo méje kojá isẹ́jú mẹ́sàn –

5.   Agogo méje kojá isẹ́jú mẹ́ta –

6.   Agogo kan kojá isẹ́jú mẹta –

116

182 White-faced mask of a type used by the BaKota, BaLumbo, BaPunu, Mpongwe and several other tribes. Documented pieces have been collected among all these peoples. Among the BaPunu the wearer dances on stilts. Rietberg Museum, Zürich. Ht 11¾ in.

183 Wooden figures covered with brass or copper sheeting are placed by the BaKota over a package containing sample bones of outstanding ancestors. Siroto suggests that the form was developed to display as much of the valuable metal as possible. Certainly its two-dimensional character attracted Western painters; Juan Gris made a copy of one in cardboard in 1922. British Museum. Ht 26 in.

7. Agogo meji kojá èséjúméje –

8. Agogo márùn kojá iséjúméjo –

9. Agogo mẹta àbọ - géré = 30 min or ½

10. Agogo mewa a bọ

11. Mókànla kojá isé jú méwà

12. Agogo mésàn ku isejúu méjo

13. Ago méjìlá kója ogún isé jú

14. Agogo kan ku iséjú méjo

15. Agogo méji kojá ogbòn isé jú

16. Agogo mẹta ló lù géèré

17. Agogo mẹta ku isé jú mẹta

CALENDAR – ÌLÀNÀ ÌKOJÓ

- Wakaiti merinlelogun ni o wa ninu ojokan **24** hours make one day.

- Ọjọ́ méje ni o wa ninu òsè kan – Seven days make one week.

- Òsè mẹ́rin ni o wa ninu osù kan – Four weeks make one month.

- Osu méjìlá ni o wa ninu odún kan – Twelve months make one year.

- Orúkọ awọn Ọjo ọse – Name of the weekdays in Yoruba.

1. Sunday – Ọjọ́ àìkú

2. Monday – Ọjọ́ ajé

3. Tuesday – Ọjọ́ ìségun

4. Wednesday – Ọjọ́ rú

5. Thursday – Ọjọ bọ

6.   Friday – Ojó ẹtì

7.   Saturday – Àbá mẹ́ta

1.   Mo lọ sí ibi isẹ́ ni ojọ́ – ajé/I went to work on Monday. (Construct another five sentences as above.)

2.   Akò ní lo sí ibi isẹ́ ni ojọ Àìkú àti ojọ́ Àbá mẹ́ta/We will not go to work on both Saturday and Sunday. (Construct your own five sentences.)

Name of the Months are calculated by ordinal numbers from 1 through 12.

1.	January – Òsu kíní Ọdún	Osù-fẹ́rẹ́
2.	February – Osù Kejì Ọdún	Osù-Ìrèlè
3.	March – Oṣù kẹ́ta Ọdún	Osù-Ẹrèna
4.	April – Oṣù Kẹrin Ọdún	Osù-Ìgbe
5.	May – Oṣù Karún Odún	Osù-Èbìbì
6.	June – Òsu Kefà Ọdún	Osù-Òkúdù
7.	July – Oṣu keje Ọdún	Osù-Agemọ
8.	August – Òsu Kejo Ọdún	Osù-Ògun
9.	September – Òsu Kesan Ọdún	Osù-Òwewé
10.	October – Oṣu Kẹ́wà Ọdún	Osù-Òwara
11.	November – Oṣu Kokànlá Ọdún	Osù-Bẹ́lú
12.	December – Oṣu Kejìlá Ọdún	Osù-Opẹ́

Example/Exercise: My friend will get married in January/Ọrẹ mi yo ṣegbeyawo ninu <u>osù kinni odun</u>. Now construct sentences as above.

How to count the days

●   Òní – Today

- Ọla – Tomorrow

- Ànań – Yesterday/ana

- Ìjẹta – Day before yesterday

- Ìjẹrin – Four days ago

- Ìjárun – Five days ago

- Ìjẹfà – Six days ago

- Ìjeje – Seven days ago

- Ìjẹjo – Eight days ago

- Ìjẹsan – Nine days ago

- Ìjẹwa – Ten days ago

- Ìjọkànlá – Eleven days ago

- Ìjejìlá – Twelve days ago

- Ìjẹtàlá – Thirteen days ago

- Ìjẹrìnlá – Fourteen days ago

- Ìjẹedógún – Fifteen days ago

- Ìjẹrìndínlógún – Sixteen days ago

- Ìjẹtàdínióógún – Seventeen days ago

- Ìjejìdínlógún – Eighteen days ago

- Ìjọkàndínlógún – Nineteen days ago

- Ogúnjọ́ Òní – Twenty days ago

- Ìjọkànlélógún – Twenty-one days ago

- Ìjẹtàlélógún – Twenty-three days ago

- Ìjẹrinlélógún – Twenty-four days ago

- Ìjẹẹdógbọn – Twenty-five days ago

- Ìjẹrindínlógbọn – Twenty-six days ago

- Ìjẹtàdínlógbọn – Twenty-seven days ago

- Ìjẹjìdínlógbọn – Twenty-eight days ago

- Ìjọkàndínlógbọn – Twenty-nine days ago

- Ogbọnjọ́ Òní – Thirty days ago

Exercise: (i.e.) Òní ni ọjọ́ ìbí mi/Today is my birthday. Construct your <u>ten</u> sentences using example above.

COUNTING BY WEEKS, MONTHS AND YEARS

- Òsè tombo – Next week

- Òsè yi – This week

- Òsù ti o koja – Last year

- Odún ti o koja – Last month

- Ọdún ni/ọdún yi – This year

- Nídunta – Year before the last or three years ago

- Nídunrin – Four years ago

- Nídunrùn– Five years ago

- Nídunfà – Six years ago

- Nídunje – Seven years ago

- Nídunjọ – Eight years ago

- Nídunsàn – Nine years ago

- Ní dunwà – Ten years ago (after the 10th year, names of years are counted by ordinal numbers.

- Odún kokanlá séhìn – Eleven years ago

- Odún kejìlá séhìn – Twelve years ago

- Odún ketàlá – Thirteen years ago

- Odún kerìnlá séhìn – Fourteen years ago

- Odún kèèédógún séhìn – Fifteen years ago

- Odún kerìndínlógún séhìn – Sixteen years ago

- Odún ketàdínlógún séhìn – Seventeen years ago

- Odún kejìndínlógún séhìn – Eighteen years ago

- Ogún odùn séhìn – Twenty years ago

- Ogbòn odún séhìn – Forty years ago

- Ogóji odún séhìn – Forty years ago

- Àádóta odún séhìn – Fifty years ago

- Àádórin odún séhìn – Seventy years ago

- Ogórin odún séhìn – Eighty years ago

- Àádórun odún séhìn – Ninety years ago

- Ogórun odùn sehin – One hundred years ago

Exercise I

Tunde was born eleven years ago/abi Tunde ni odun kokanla sehin. Now construct <u>ten</u> sentences using the above example.

Exercise II

1.   What is the English of this Yorùbá day "ojó àìkú"?

a) Monday
b) Sunday
c) Tuesday

2. Which one of these is the correct day of "Ojọ́ etì"?

a) Friday
b) Saturday
c) Wednesday

3. Which of these days come immediately after ojọ́rú?

a) Thursday
b) Monday
c) Sunday

4. Which of these months is the eleventh month?

a) Oṣù kẹta ọdún/Oṣù Erèna
b) Oṣù Irele
c) Oṣù kokànlá ọdún/Oṣù bẹ́lú

5. Which of these is the correct word for "Lánàa"? (or) ànàn

a) Yesterday
b) Today
c) Last year
d) Last week

6. How many days make a week? Write your answer in Yoruba words.

7. How many weeks make a month? Write your answer in Yoruba words.

8. How many months make a leap year? Write your answer in Yoruba words.

9. Name these months in English.

a) Oṣù Igbe
b) Oṣu Agẹmọ
c) Osù Erèna
d) Osù Ebìbì
e) Osù Òkúdù

123

10. Name these months in Yorùbá ordinal form. (i.e.) Osù kejì odún

   a) January
   a) May
   b) June
   c) August
   d) December

96. *Bronze head, Bini (Benin Kingdom), Nigeria*
14"

NOUNS DENOTES THE NAME OF PERSON, PLACE AND THINGS

The chief subjects of verbs in sentences are <u>nouns</u>. Nouns can also be the objects of verbs, or prepositions, or of verbals, as complements following a linking verb, as appositives or modifiers or other words. In Yorùbá, the nouns don't necessarily change their form to show number by adding -s, es, as in the English language, a noun may designate a person's name such as Àkàndé, Adélékè, Òkánlàwón, Àdùké, Àjàlá, Babátúndé, and so on. Yorùbá nouns may also designate things, such as television, sinima, storybook, burned bread, pencil, and so on. Nouns can also designate quality such as beauty, ugly, and rage. Nouns may designate action such as hunting, eating, and so on, or ideas such as justice, reality, love, wisdom and so on.

There are no inflections for gender, number, person and case in Yorùbá. As for number, the pronoun "awon" is sometimes added to the noun to denote plurality; however, this is not an invariable rule. A word may be understood to denote plurality with or without pronounce "àwon." See the following examples:

FORMS, FUNCTIONS AND CLASSES OF YORÙBÁ NOUNS

1.   **SINGULAR**   **PLURAL**

1.   Boy – òdómokùnrin   Boys – Àwon òdómokùnrin

2.   Girl – òdómobìnrin   Girls – Àwon òdómobìnrin

3.   Child – omodé   Children – Àwon omodé

3 Dance headdress, in the form of an antelope with young, representing the spirit *chi wara* who introduced agriculture to the Bambara. These headdresses, attached to a wickerwork cap, are worn in pairs by young men of the *flankuru* or co-operating group of farmers who at the time of planting and harvest dance in imitation of a leaping antelope. British Museum. Ht 31¼ in.

4.	Baby – ìkókoó	Babies – Àwọn ìkókoó
5.	Man – ọkùnrin	Men – Àwọn ọkùnrin
6.	Woman – obìnrin	Women – Àwọn obìnrin
7.	Student – akékò	Students – Àwọn akékò
8.	Book – ìwé	Books – Àwọn ìwé
9.	Friend – òré	Friends – Àwọn òré
10.	Cat – ológbò	Cats – Àwọn ológbò

Again, in Yorùbá language the plural nouns are noticed by the word "àwọn" that precedes the noun. Also, there is no 'an' before vowel sounds as in English (i.e.), "an egg."

2.   COMPOUND NOUNS OR GROUP WORDS

In Yorùbá language, ther are two or more nouns written as one word, as two words, or hyphenated that function as a single unit. Some of these are:

Bookcase – àpótí ìwe

Football – bólù àfesègbá

Pineapple – òpọn òyìnbó

High School – ilé ìwé gíga

Police Officer – ògá ọlópà

Attorney General – amòfin àgbà

3.   (POSSESSIVE NOUNS) IN YORUBA THE WORD "TI AWỌN" WITHOUT ELISION "T" AWỌN SIGNIFIES

Possessive nouns (without elision)
Boys' – t'àwọn òdómọkùnrin

127

18 Drum from the Baga, in a style rather
different from that seen in the *demba* mask, in
Ill. 17. This type of drum has been said to be
used in funeral ceremonies but this is unlikely
to be its only use. British Museum. Ht 44 in.

Girls' – t'àwọn obìnrin

Mens' – t'àwọn ọkùnrin

Cats' – t'àwon ológbò

Dogs' – t'àwọn ajá

4. COLLECTIVE NOUNS

Collective nouns take singular or plural verbs depending on the meaning. What is a collective noun? A collective noun has singular form but names a group of individual things. Here are some examples:

Army – Àwọn ọmọ ogun

Audience – Agbo

Committee Ìgbìmò/ìpàdé alábe sékélé

Family – Ìdílé

Group/club – Ẹgbẹ́

Team-mate – Ọmọ eléré kán ńa

When used as a subject, a Yorùbá collective noun may take a singular or plural verb, depending on the context in which it appears. However, when you are considering the groups as a unit, use the singular form of the verb. Example: síbèsíbè, ìdílé onígbàgbó tuń dúró gboin gboin ni Nigeria. This means: the Nigerian Christian family is still strong.

"Any band sounds good in that concert hall." – Gbogbo òsèré ló má ńse dádá ninu gbògàn eré ńa.

The ladies from Nigeria

5. LOCATIVE NOUNS 'IBI' 'ILÉ' 'ÒDÒ'

"Òdò" is used before a possessive pronoun like 'mi', 'rẹ', 'mẹ̀nẹ̀ me, his/hers.

Examples of the use of "òdò":

1. Láyí wà ní òdò mi/Láyí is with me.

2. Túndé lo sí òdò rẹ̀/Túndé has gone to him/her

3. Mò/nlọ sí òdò olùkó/I'm going to the teacher

    This locative noun "ọdọ" can also precede any relative pronouns, such as:

    Ọ̀dọ̀ tani o wà?/ Who have you been with?

    Ọ̀dọ̀ tani bún lọ?/Who are you going to?

    'Ilé' simply means "house": but it is used many times as a pronoun. That is

'ilé' can be used to refer to places of activities. Examples of the use of "ilé."

1. Mò nlo sí ilé – I am going home. Here "ilé" is used as a dwelling place.

2. Mò nlo sí ilé ìfowópamó – I am going to the bank. Here "ilé" is used as a pre-noun and as a place of activity.

3. Mò nlo sí ilé iṣé – I am going to work. This is the same when we say: Mò nló sí ibi isé, which also means, "I am going to work."

Example – Ọ̀dọ̀ – Mo fé lọ sí òdò Túndé/I want to go to 'Túndé

1. Mo fé – I want

2. Lọ sí òdò – to go to

3. 'Túndé – 'Túndé (a name)
    Mo fé lọ sí òdò Túndé

1. Now match "mo fé lọ sí 'òdò' with the names below. Mo fé lọ sí òdò, I want

to go. To Write i.e. Mo fẹ́ lọ sí ọ̀dọ̀ ____. (Choose a name below to fill in the blank.)

Kúnlé	Títí	Dayọ̀
Bádé	Kíké	Bùnmi
Soji	Fúnmi	Adé
Táíwò	Yẹmí	Akin
Bímpé	Lọlá	Tóbi

2. Sí 'ilé' or si 'ibi'

Example: Mò ńlọ sí Ilé ìwé – I am going to school. Match the following places with either mò ńlo si ibi or mo nlo si ilé.

1. Iṣẹ́ – work
2. Ijó – dance
3. Eré – game
4. Elẹ́ran – meat seller (butcher)
5. Ilé ẹjọ́ – courthouse

6. Oti – beer
7. Àṣe – Party
8. Igbeyawo – wedding venue
9. Ile Olórun – church
10. Aladura – prophet

132

Formation of Nouns in Yorùbá

Nouns formed by Reproduction

1. Nouns are formed from verbs by reduplicating the first syllable of the verb.

    Example:

Verbs	Reduplicated Verbs
1. Dára/good	Dídára – goodness
2. Múję/eat	Mímúnję – act of eating
3. Sa ló/run away	Sísálọ – the act of running
4. Tun ṣé/repair	Títunṣe – the act of being repaired
5. Tóbi/great	Títóbi – greatness

2. **Nouns formed by reduplication form transitive verb**

    Examples:

    1. Títa – that which is for sale

    2. Ríra – that which is to be brought

    3. Gígùn – the length of

    4. Fífọ – that which is to be washed

    5. Kíkùn – that which is to be printed

3. **Nouns formed by reduplicating a noun**

    Examples:

Nouns	Reduplicated Nouns
Èdè – language	Èdèkédè – any language
Eiye – bird	Eiyekéye – any bird
Ọmọ – child	Ọmọkómọ – any child
Owó – money	Owókówó – any money
Obìnrin – woman	Obìnrinkóbìnrin – any woman
Ènìyàn – person	Enikéni – any person
Ọmọ – child	Ọmọ olómọ – another person's child
Ayé – life	Ayeraye – everlasting
Owó – hand	Ọwódówó – hand to hand
Ti Ìran – geneology/generation	Àtìrandéran – from generation to generation
Ilé – house	Ilékílé – any house

4. **Nouns formed by composition**

In this case two nouns are occasionally compounded together, the processor or the qualifying term being placed last, this is the reverse of English order.

Examples: ile-tubu, Ile-house-tubu-jail, house of jail. (Jailhouse)

1.	Aṣọ-òkè	The traditional special Yorùbá attire
2.	Ọmọ-èhìn	Follower/disciples

3.	Ẹni ọ̀wọ̀	Reverend
4.	Ọmọ- òdò	Houseboy/girl
5.	Ojú-ọ̀nàn	The eyes of the road, the main road
6.	Ilé-ejọ́	Courthouse
7.	Olùsọ́-àgùtàn	A minister/shepherd

5. **Sometimes a whole phrase is frequently united to form a <u>noun phrase</u>.**

Examples:

1.	Afibisólóore	Ungrateful person
2.	Alágàbàgebè	Double dealer or hypocrite
3.	Alábòsí	Traitor
4.	Olófòfó	Gossiper
5.	Alásejù	Very demanding individual
6.	Aláầnú	Merciful person
7.	Aláiláầnú	Merciless person
8.	Alásìrí	Dependable person
9.	Aláìnítìjú	Shameless person
10.	Aláìrí rònú	Thoughtless person

6. **Many nouns in 'a' are compounded with verbs to <u>form new abstract nouns</u>.**

Examples:

1.	Àsálà	Escape
2.	Àféṭán	Perfect love
3.	Ìdùnnú	Happiness
4.	Ìyèdún	Surviving the year
5.	Àlàjá	A successful end

Exercise 1

1. What is a collective noun? Give three examples.

2. Write five examples of locative nouns.

3. Distinguish between collective nouns and compound nouns; give two examples of each.

4. Write three nouns formed by composition and two formed by

   reduplication.

5. What is an abstract noun? Give four examples of abstract nouns.

6. Group these nouns below into (a) noun phrases (b) abstract nouns; afibisólóre, alágàbàngebè, àsálà, ìdùnnú, àlàjá, ìyèdún.

7. State two ways of knowing plural nouns; give two examples.

8. State five nouns formed by reduplicating, and five formed by

   compositions.

9. Explain what you know about gender, and it's relationship to nouns.

10. Indicate the type of nouns these words are: Àkàndé, 040, U.S.A., beauty, bottle, wisdom, cat and dog.

136

Exercise 2

Directions: Draw a picture of yourself and label accordingly.

1. Mo fọwọ kán irun mi/I touched my hair.

    Òjó, fọwọ́ kan irun rẹ̀/Òjó touch my hair.

2. Mo, Fọ̀ kan etí mi/I touched my ear.

    Àiná, Fowó Kan etí re/Àiná touch my ear.

3. Mo Fowó kan ojú mi/I touched my eye.

    Àjàyí, Fọwọ́ Kan Ojú re/Àjàyí, touch your eye.

4. Mo Fọwọ́ kan imú mi/I touched my nose.

    Dàda, Fọwọ́ kan imú re/Dàda, touch your nose.

5. Mo Fọwọ́ kan ẹnu mi/I touched my mouth.

6. Mo Fọwọ́ kan ojúngun mi/I touched my calf.

    Ẹ̀taòkò, fowó kan ojúngun re/Ẹ̀taòkò, touch my calf.

7. Mo Fowó kan àtẹ́lesẹ̀ mi.

    I touched my toes, ilori, fowo kan atelesere/Ìlòrí touch your toes.

8. I touched my head/Ewéjé touch your head.

9. Mo Fowó kan itan mi/I touched my chest.

    Ifásèyí, fowó kan àyà re/Ifásèyí, touch your chest.

10. Mo Fowó kan ìgbùnwó mi/I touched my elbow.

    Efúnseun, fowó kan ìgbùnwó re/Efúnseun, touch your elbow.

APPOSITION

When nouns are in apposition, the principal word comes first; as in:

137

- Ẹ̀mí ni Ọlọ́run – God is Spirit

- Aláànú ni Ọlọ́run – God is merciful

- Ọlọgbọ́n ni ọ́ – You are a wise person

- Alágbára ni bàbá mi – My father is powerful

Mr Joe Keshi

Label the Picture below accordingly.

AWON EYA ARA – PARTS OF THE BODY

orí - head _____   _____ irun - hair

iwájú - forehead _____   _____ etí - ear

ehín - teeth _____   _____ ojú - eye

àyà - chest _____   _____ imú - nose

ìgbùnwó - elbow _____   _____ èrèké - cheek

ikùn - abdomen _____   _____ ẹnu - mouth

ìka owo - fingernails _____ _____ ọyàn - breast

orúkún - knee _____   _____ apá - arm

èékánná - toenail _____   _____ ọwọ́ - hand

àgbòn - cheek _____   _____ itan - thigh

orùn - neck _____   _____ ojúgun - shin

                                       _____ ẹsẹ̀ - foot

                                       _____ àtẹ́lẹsẹ̀ - toe

                                       _____ gìgísẹ̀ - heel

What is a pronoun?

1.   A pronoun is a word which cannot have a qualifier in the nominal group.

Pronouns have a system of number (singular and plural) of person (i.e.)

(1ˢᵗ, 2ⁿᵈ, 3ʳᵈ person). They also have different forms for the different

syntactic positions.

I.   Pronoun Subject

	a.	Singular	Plural
	1.	mo	a
	2.	o	ẹ
	3.	ọ́	n
	4.	ngó/unó	nwọn

2.   Before the verbal particle n, the first and second person pronouns have

alternative form. This form has a low tone, (i.e.) Mo, o, a, ẹ, (e.g.) Mo ńlọ

(I am going). Before the verb form a will, the subject pronoun does.

	b.	Singular			Plural	
	1.	Mǎ	I will	ǎ	we will
	2.	Wàá	You will	ẹ	you all will
	3.	á	He/she	nwon	they
c.	Màá lọ	–	I will go
	Wàá lọ	–	You will go
	Á á lọ	–	She/he will go

45 Terracotta head found by gold-miners in the Mokuro Stream, Ife. The bulging eyes, flat protrusive lips and stylized ears indicate its intermediate position between the naturalistic style of ancient Ife sculpture and that of Yoruba works of the present day. Ife Museum. Ht 7¾ in.

Exercise:

1.   List the singular and plural pronoun subject.

2.   On a "T" table differentiate subject pronoun series in both singular and plural.

3.   Subjective Case of Pronouns in Yorùbá

Pronouns are subjects of verbs. In Yorùbá, you can use the subjective case of pronouns when the pronouns are the subject of verb just as in the English language.

a.	I saw the bird	Mo rí'ẹyiẹ
b.	He enjoys dancing	O fẹran ijó
c.	We bought the car	A rá oko na
d.	They are fighting over the girls	Nwón ńjà ńitoríobìnrin nâ

4.   The Use of Objective Case

Pronouns cannot be linked by "àti", and they cannot occur before certain verbs such as "dà" where is? "Nkò" what about? "Ko" isn't and "ni" is.

a.   Pronoun Object

Singular		Plural
1.	Mi	Wa
2.	o/ẹ	Nyín
3.	a vowel of verb	Wọn

5.   The tone of the pronoun objects depend on that of the preceding verb. It is

40 Mask cast from almost pure copper in the naturalistic style for which Ife art is best known. This piece was clearly intended to be worn, perhaps in the burial rituals of a king of Ife. It is said always to have been kept on a shrine in the palace, and thus was for a long time the only example of Ife metal-casting known in the town. It is not surprising, therefore, that it was thought to represent Obalufon who is supposed to have introduced the technique to Ife. Ife Museum. Ht 13 in.

41 A group of highly stylized heads from various parts of Ife which appear to be contemporary with heads in an intensely naturalistic style. The second from the left shows a blend of a conical head shape and moderately naturalistic features. Ife Museum. Hts 5, 7½, 6½, 6¾ in.

mid tone after the high verb, and a high tone after a mid or low tone verb.

e.g.

Ó rí mi   He saw me

Ó jọ mí   He resembles me

Ó wò mí   He looked at me

Ó gbà á   He got it

The 2nd person plural pronoun object, however, always goes a higher tone.

Exercise:

1.   List and show five subjective cases of pronouns.

2.   Demonstrate the use of objective cases in both singular and plural.

RELATIVE PRONOUNS

6.   The relatives "ti" who or which is applied to both persons and things, and

is not varied to indicate gender, number, or case "ti" is usually followed by

O or O.

1.   These are generally used for all numbers and persons.

"O"

1.   Àwa tí "Ó" wá – we who come

2.   Àwa tí "Ó" rí – we who see

3.   Àwa tí "Ó" mọ̀ – we who know

4.   Kíkọ̀ tí O kọ̀ = by your refusal

5.   Ẹ̀kọ́ tí O kọ́ = the knowledge that you acquired

319. 9"

320. 11"

321. 10"

322. 9"

323. 6"

324. 7"

325. 6"

326. Cup with ivory
head and wood base. 9"

6.   Bámi tọ́ lọ = go to him for me (third person)

2.   Relative pronouns cannot be governed directly by a preposition, but only through a noun or pronoun as in:

  1.   Fún ẹni tí = to whom or for whom

  2.   Fún ẹni kẹ́ni = to who ever

  3.   Fún ẹnì kan = for someone

3.   The possessive case is expressed: If we can employ a personal pronoun, that must follow the name of the things possessed.

  1.   Ọkùnrin tí O ṣẹ̀sẹ̀ ra ilé = the man who just bought a house

  2.   Ọkùnrin tí ilé rẹ jó = the man whose house was burnt

  3.   Obìnrin tí nwón lu omo rẹ̀ = the lady whose child was beaten

Exercise:

1.   What are the Yorùbá particles for relative pronouns?

2.   Demonstrate the use of one of them in three sentences.

7.   The Use of Pre-Subject Pronouns in Yorùbá "jẹ́kí"

*If you want to ask for the company of friends to do something, you will start as follows:

  Ẹjẹ́ ká = let us

  Ẹjẹ́ kó = let him or her

96 Commander William Allen's drawing of the Ata of Igala in 1832–33. He is wearing a mask round his neck which Allen described as 'a gilt representation – or libel – of the human face, very like the "man in the moon"'.

Ẹjẹ́ kí won = let them

Ẹjẹ́ kín = let me

EXERCISE

* Now match each of these pre-subject pronouns with the following verbs (i.e., ẹjẹ́ ká jọ- (let's dance). Place ejeka before the following verbs in order to construct a complete sentence.

_____   Lo = let us go

_____   Sùn = sleep (let us sleep)

_____   Dáké = (let us be quiet)

_____   Jeun = eat (let us eat)

_____   Pàtéwó = clap (let us clap)

_____   Seré = play (let us play)

_____   Rí = see (let us see it)

_____   Báelo = go with you (let us go with)

_____   Seé = do it (let us do it)

_____   Korin = sing (let us sing)

8.   Gerund: Verbs Used as Nouns

The gerund in English is a noun created from the -ing form of a verb. Like other nouns, gerunds act as subjects and objects in sentences.

Examples:

Singing lifts me up   →   Orin ńfún mi láyọ̀

148

232 An elaborate bowl carved about 1925 by Olowe. The head between the supporting figures is completely separate from the rest of the sculpture. Formerly Coll. William J. Moore. Ht 25 in.

Wrestling is dangerous	➜	Ìjàkadì léwu
Waiting can be boring	➜	Ìdúró a má sọkàn lâarè
Going seems rough	➜	Ìtèsíwájú le or (sòro)
Sleeping can be relaxing	➜	Oorún le fún nı ní ìtura
Laughing can be rewarding	➜	Èrè ŵa nínú èrín
Giving has no seasons	➜	Ore kò ní ìgbà

THE NOUN HEAD

There are certain junction features between a noun head; Its noun head is lengthened on a mid tone before a consonant initial noun and before all pronouns, except the first and second person singular, e.g.

1. Ilée bàbá   Father's house

    Ilée wa   Our house

    Ajáa Délé   Délé's dog

Other junction features may be illustrated by the following examples:

2. Òrò asọ>oroo aso   talk about dress

    Sòòsì oko>sóòsì oko   village church

    Èrò won>èròò won   their thoughts

A noun or pronoun qualifier can be in apposition to the noun head, e.g.

3. Àwa Yorùbá   We Yorubas

    Dókítà Òyìnbó   European Doctor

    Gbogboo wa   All of us

4.   The pronominal as the head, followed by a noun in apposition is very common. The 3rd person plural form of it (followed by a noun) is used for indicating that there is more than one of the nouns referred to. (NOTE: A noun without a qualifier can stand for one or more pronominals).

For example:

	Pro nominal		Noun in Apposition	
Ìyàwó	Wife	Àwọn Ìyàwó		Wives
Ọmọ	Child	Àwọn ọmọ		Children

5.   A noun or pronoun qualifier may be in genitival relation with the noun head, e.g.

Ilé ọba	The king's house
Ojú mi	My eyes
Ọwọ́ epo	Oily hand (successful person) Idiomatic expression

There is a genitival particle <u>ti</u> that may be prefixed to a noun or pronoun in genitival relation with the noun head, e.g.

6.   Pronoun Qualifiers preceded by "ti" are:

Singular	**Plural**
1. tèmi	Tiwa
2. tèmi	Tiyín
3. tèmi	Tiwọn

(Note that pronoun qualifiers cease to behave like pronouns when they are preceded by ti.) Apart from single-word qualifiers such as nouns, pronouns, and pronominals, the qualifiers of a noun head may also be a noun with one or more qualifiers. All the features typical of the single-word qualifier are also typical of this kind of qualifier, e.g. Ilé bàbá wa (ilée bàbáawa) our father's house/Ìwọ ńiyawô mi. You are my wife. Àwọn ọ̀rẹ́ wa (àwọn ọ̀rẹ́ẹ wa) our friends. Àsà tàwon òyinbó. European customs.

7. The Use of Indirect Objects

    1.   Ìdòwú gave her the office key – Ìdòwú <u>fúun</u> ni kọ́kọ́rọ́ ilé iṣẹ́.

    2.   'Bọla gave her some food – Bọ́lá <u>fúnn</u> ni ouńjẹ

    3.   'Ṣeun helped her to fix it – Ṣeun <u>báa</u> ṣé

    4.   Tolú gave her a gift – Tolú <u>fúun</u> ńí ẹ̀bùn

    5.   'Fuńmi helped him –'Fuńmi <u>ràan</u> lọ́wọ́

    6.   Ṣeun did it for her – Ṣeun <u>bá</u> a ṣé

* The underlined above are indirect objects.

8. Direct Object

    1.   <u>The ball</u> hit him unawares – <u>bọ́lu na</u> ba lójijì

    2.   The <u>visitor</u> showed up unnoticed – <u>Àlejò</u> na de lójijì

    3.   Òjò de ba wọn lójijì – The <u>rain</u> hit them unaware

9. The demonstrative pronouns single out what you are talking about:

    1.   This   èyí

    2.   That   ìyẹn

3.   These   àwọn wọ̀n yí

4.   Those   àwọn wọ̀n yẹn or àwọn wòn ǹi

Exercise:

1.   Differentiate between the use of direct objects and indirect objects. Construct three sentences to support your answer.

2.   List four demonstrative pronouns you know. Remember the demonstrative are placed immediately after the nouns they define, (e.g.)

<u>this</u> house   ilé <u>y̌i</u>

<u>that</u> house   ilé <u>yen</u>

<u>those</u> houses   ilé <u>wòn yen</u> or ilé <u>wòn ǹi</u>

10.   <u>Demonstrative pronounce</u>. When the noun is followed by a demonstrative word, the demonstrative is placed after both: (e.g.)

1.   <u>That</u> man of courage   Ọkùnrin oní̱gboyà <u>nâ</u>

2.   <u>That</u> good person   Ènìyàn rere <u>nâ</u>

3.   <u>That</u> heroic man   Ọkùnrïn akin <u>nâ</u>

Both "yen and "na" may be attached to plural nouns as:

4.   Àwọn ẹranko yẹn   Those animals

        Gbogobo aṣọ nâ   All the cloth

When the demonstratives are employed substantively, they are augmented by the addiction of the usual performatives as:

5.   Èyí, or eléyǐ/this   èyí dára   this is good

       The plural of these are

6.   Àwǒn yi, ìwònyí/these   Àwọn yẹn/those

Sometimes "èyí" reduplicates the second syllable; as: èyíyǐ – this; and

frequently it is compounded with "ni", forming the compound substantive

pronoun "èyí ni" meaning this is it.

       "Òn nǎ" "àwọn na" are empathatic, as Àwọn ná nì mo fẹ́ – those

are what I want (plural)

       Òn ná nì mo fẹ́, that is the one I want (singular)

Define Article

1.   "Na" – always refers to "that" or "the" as okùnrin nǎ/the man,

       alágbára ni okùnrin nâ/the man is powerful.

2.   Ni – means "it is" in English i.e. oba ni/It is the king.

3.   Èyí – "as this," is employed as definite article as in, èyí ni a rí –

       That is what we saw.

       Èyí dára – that is good.

       Èyí pòjù – that is too much.

       Èyí lẹ́wa – this is beautiful.

       Èyí wùwá - we admire this.

Commands are easier to construct than questions. When forming commands, we merely delete the subject of the sentence, such as you (Ìwo).

Instead of open the door – <u>Iwo silekun</u>, we look at the person and say:

Dayọ̀ sílèkun	Dayọ̀ – open the door
Dayọ̀ jókòó	Dayọ̀ – sit down
Dayọ̀ wá ní bí	Dayọ̀ – come over or come here
Dayọ̀ kọ orin	Dayọ̀ – sing

When command is given to several people or to an older person, one must use the homonic pronoun before the verbs.

Example: The word can be used to address all of you (or for an elderly person).

Formal:	Ẹ wá	Come
	Ẹ sùn	Sleep
	Ẹ dìde	Stand up
	E jókòó	Sit down

The verb "má" or "Má se" may be used to form the negative imperative. Both "má" and "má se" means the same thing.

Informal:	Má sùn lọ	don't sleep off
	Má tíi jèun	don't eat yet
	Má tàn mí je	don't deceive me

16. *Ceremonial pottery jar, Mangbetu, Congo. 13"*

"má ṣe" and "ma" means don't in English language, for example, ma –don't and

má ṣe –do not.

Exercise – Isé ṣíse

Form ten questions and ten commands from the following nouns and verbs on the

next page. Using Tìtí, Délé, Kíké, Fúnmi,'Láyí, Kúnlé, Mímì, Tópé, Búkỳ, Adé,

and other names of your choice.

The word "jòwó" / "please", is added after the noun or pronouns. For

example: Kúnlé jòwó wá – Kunle please come

Adé jòwó kàwé/adé please read

Exercise #1

Now command these people politely as above. Remember to use the

names before the word "please" and then the verb. You may choose from the

following names: (Bádé, Ọlá, Túnjí, Kọ́lá, Tìtí, Mímì, Délé, Fúnmi, Bímpé) (i.e.),

Ọlá jọwọ wòkè – Ọla please look up. Match the appropriate English command

that are provided below.

Example: Ọlá jòwó wòkè (Ọlá please look up)

_____	Gbà	Take
_____	Dúró	Waite
_____	Kà'wé	Read
_____	Fi mí sílè	Leave me alone
_____	Kúrò ní bí	Get out of here

22 Mask made by the Fang, given in 1905 to Maurice Vlaminck who sold it to André Derain. It was seen also by Picasso and Matisse. This was not the first African sculpture to attract Vlaminck, but it appears to be the only one from this time which is still certainly identifiable. Musée National d'Art Moderne, Paris. Ht $18\frac{7}{8}$ in.

_____	Di ojú rẹ	Close your eyes
_____	Fún mi ní tèmi	Give me mine
_____	Si íwe rẹ	Open your book
_____	Gbàdúrà	Pray
_____	Dákẹ́	Be quiet

Exercise #2

You can form the negative imperative of the above by putting "mase" on "ma" in front of the verb.

Example:

Adé jọwọ́ máṣe wòkè – Adé please don't look up or

Adé jọwọ́ má wòkè – Ade please don't look up

Now compose ten negative imperative of the above by putting "má se" or "má" before the verbs, just as demonstrated above.

GENDER FORMATION

1. Most Yorùbá nouns do not have different gender for masculine and feminine: such as actor and actress, chairman and chairlady as in English language. However, many English readers prefer to use some of the feminine forms to address females, such as poetess, authoress, directress, and so on. In Yoruba language, the gender of the actor or player is declared by gender identity such as female actress or male actress.

MALE	FEMALE	MALE	FEMALE
Actor	Actress	Òsèré Okùnrim	Òsèré Obìnrin
Teacher	Mistress	Olùkó Okùnrin	Olùko Obìnrin
Prophet	Prophetess	Wòlíì Okunrin	Wolii Obìnrin
Chairman	Chairlady	Alága Okùnrin	Alága Obìnrin

2.   Again, Yoruba nouns do not express gender, number, or case; in other words, they exhibit no traces of inflexion. Gender is distinguished only where there is an actual difference of sex as follows:

ANIMAL GENDERLIZATION

MALE	FEMALE
Ako – he animal	Abo – she animal
Àkùko – a cock	Àgbébò – hen
Àgbò or oko – a he goat	Àké – a she goat
Àko esin – a he horse	Abo esin – a she horse or mare
Lion/Ekùn – a he lion	Lioness – Abo ekùn

HUMAN GENDERLIZATION

MALE	FEMALE
Okùnrin	Obìnrin – a woman
Bàbá – father	Ìyá – mother
Egbón okùnrin – an elder brother	Egbón obìnrin – an elder sister
Àbúrò okùnrin – a younger brother	Àbúrò obìnrin – a younger sister
Báálé (oba ilé) – father of a family	Ìya'lé – mother of family

32 Polychrome painting of a disguised Bushman hunting ostriches at Witteberge, Herschel, Cape Province, South Africa. W. 26 in. (After Stow and Bleek.)

head of household

Balógun – a general (ọba nínú ogun)   Iyalase – a female cook

Exercise:

In a "T" table supply the following feminine genders. Remember to write the

Yorùbá form for each.

Male Gender	**Female Gender**
1. Òṣèré Ọkùnrin/actor	_____
2. Olùkọ́ Ọkùn rin/male teacher	_____
3. Wòlíî/prophet	_____
4. Alága Okùnrin/chairman	_____
5. Balógun/a general	_____
6. Baálé/head of household	_____
7. Ọkùnrin/man	_____
8. Bàbá/father	_____
9. Ègbọ́n okùnrin/elder brother	_____
10. Àbúrò Okùnrin/younger brother	_____
11. Àkùko/a cook	_____
12. Akọ/he (or) male	_____
13. Àgbò/a he goat	_____
14. A he horse/akọ ẹshin	_____
15. Ẹkùn/lion	_____

211 Staff carried by a devotee, from the Temple of Shongo, the thunder god, in Ogbomosho. This sculpture shows the aesthetic qualities which characterize Yoruba sculpture. National Museum of African Art, Washington, D.C. Ht 16½ in.

Most Yorùbá meals are tasty and prepared hot. The Yorùbá seldomly eat cold meals. For meats, they have goat, cow, chicken, turkey, geese, guinea fowls, pigeon, fish, shrimp, and crab. Others are deer, snake, bushrat, crocodiles, antelope, rams, squirrels, snails, tiger, and most birds, including ducks, but Yoruba people do not eat cats, dogs, monkeys or babooms, frogs, lizards, house rats and cameleons.

FRUIT GROUP

Fruits and vegetables eaten in Yoruba are: oranges, bananas, pineapples, tangerines, carrots, watermelons, guava, melons, limes, grapefruits, mangos, apple (these apples are not like American apples). They are tinier, and pink and white in color, peppers, tomatoes, onions, peas and many other edible fruits.

THE OIL GROUP AND TYPES OF FOOD

A popular oil used for cooking is called palm oil, which is a reddish colored oil made from group palm kernels, groundnut oil, melon oil and olive oil. Some of the more common Yoruba foods include: White Rice, Jollof Rice, Red Soup, Ègúsí, Beans, Boiled Yam, Pounded Yam, Plantain, Àmàlà, Èbà.

White Rice

Rinse rice in a bowl.
Put rice in a pot and add 6 cups of water. Add salt.
Place rice on stove and let cook until done.
Drain any remaining water.
Serves: 4-6. Can be eaten with any soup.

The Food Pyramid
Eka awon Onje

The Food Guide Pyramid is a general guide that lets you choose a healthy diet that is right for you. The Pyramid calls for eating a variety of foods to get the nutrients you need and eatting the right amount of calories to maintain a healthy weight. Most calories should come from foods in the three lower sections of the Pyramid.

Eka orisirisi awon onje ati àpèjúwe re jeki ale yan awon onje ti o dara fun wa. Eka onje yi fun wa ni alafia lati yan orisirisi awon onje ti onse ara ni alafia ti oye, lati maje ati lati mo iwon kalori ti o dara fun ilera ara. Opo kalori ni lati wa inu onje ti owa ni isale abe eka meta ninu awon eka onje yi.

Each of these groups provide not all, of the nutrients you need. one group can not replace those i No one food group is more impo: another. For good health, you ne

Ikan ninu awon apejuwe onje wo alaye die ninu awon ohun ti owu osi se pataki ninu ara wa. Onje i apejuwe kokan wonyi kole paro ninu apejuwe miran. Kosi onje l apejuwe wonyi ti o se pataki ju a Fun ilera pipe ati alafia, gbogbo lo wulo fun wa.

Fats, Oils, and Sweets
Use Sparingly

Malo awon nkan wonyi pe
Epo ati iyo didun.

Meat, Poultry, Fis
Dry Beans, Eggs, :
2 - 3 Servings

Eran, Adiye, Eyi

Eja Ewa gbigbe
orisirisi epa iw

Milk, Yogurt, and Cheese
2-3 Servings

Omi oyan malu, yogoti,
ati wara iwon meji
si merin.

Vegetables
3 - 5 Servings
Efo iwon meta
si marun.

Fruit
2 - 4
Eso
n

Bread, Cereal, Rice, and Pasta   6 - 11 Servings
Buredi, cereal, iresi, ati pasita iwon mefa si
mokanla.

Women are pounding yam

167

Jollof Rice

Rinse rice thoroughly.
Place rice in a pot of water and cook for 15 minutes. (Rice should not be well done).
Place oil in fry pan on low heat.
Cut ends of plantain, then cut vertically to peel off skin.
Cut plantain diagonally to desired size.
When oil is hot put plantain in until brown in color.
Then turn plantains over to other side until brown.
Remove using spatula or spoon.
Serves 6-8. Can be eaten with any kind of rice.

Àmàlà

Bring water to boil.
Add amala into water slowly while stirring.
Keep adding until thick and consistent in texture.
Serves 4. Can be eaten with any kind of soup.

Èbà

Bring water to boil.
Lower heat.
Place water into bowl and add gari.
Cover for about 2 minutes.
Use wooden spoon to stir until thick.
Serves 4. Can be eaten with any soup.
Products from yam (Tuber).

Yam:	Àmàlà – Elubl brown yam flour Iyan – Pounded yams, white yam flour Dundu – Fried Yam Ebe or Asaro – Grounded with yam seasoning
Rice:	Flour – It is prepared like pounded yam flour Boiled Rice – Jollof rice *This is the Yoruba common food.
Cassava:	Cassava – Flour (Lafun or paki) Àmàlà – Láfuń – cassava flour Iyań – cassava – cassava pounded Gàrí – cassava – fried cassava Sàkádà – cassava cake

HOW TO PREPARE JOLLOF RICE

Blend tomatoes and peppers together in a blender
Add tomato/pepper mixture and sliced onions into pot
Add water or meat broth to rice to allow rice to complete cooking
Add salt and Maggie curnes for delicious taste
Allow rice to cook completely
Serves 8. Can be eaten with red soup and plantains.

Red Soup

Blend tomatoes, peppers and onions
Heat palm oil in pot, and add tomato/pepper/onion mixture. (Color should be red).
Let cook until oil rises to the top
In separate pot, boil your choice of meat
Add meat, meat broth, crushed pepper, salt and Maggie cubes to red mixture
If soup is thick, add water
Let cook for 15 minutes
Serves 6-8.

Egúsi

Chop spinach if required
Boil choice of meat until tender and set it aside
Blend tomatoes, peppers and onions
Place the mixture, salt, Maggie cubes, oil, chopped spinach and ground engusi in pot
Let cook for 15-20 minutes
Serves 6-8.

Beans or Black Eyed Peas

Rinse beans
Ground tomatoes and pepper and set aside
In pot, add beans, mixture and sliced onions
Add salt and crushed pepper to desired taste
Cook beans until soft enough to eat
Serves 6-8. Can be eaten by itself or with white rice, bread or yams.

Pounded Yams

Slice and peel yams
Rinse thoroughly
Place yams in pot with water and let boil until tender
Drain excess water
Put in blender with little water and blend into soft dough
Serves 6-8. Can be eaten with red soup, egusi or any kind of soup.

Exercise:

1.   Explain the process of cooking and recipes of the following soup (a) ègúsí soup and (b) red soup

2.   What are the process of making
        a)   Àmàlà
        b)   Iyán
        c)   Ẹ̀bà

3.   What is your Yoruba favorite food? Why do you like it?

1.   What is a verb? In English language, a verb is the part of speech that expresses existence, action or occurrence. In Yorùbá, the verbal roots consists of a consonant and a vowel (i.e.) Yorùbá language has numerous roots of this kind. They establish the basis for the formation of nouns, adjectives and adverbs. Nouns are formed from verbal roots by the addition of appropriate vowels as prefixes. Adjectives are also formed in the manner described above. Adverbs are formed from adjectives by reduplicating the verb or adjective.

In Yorùbá, the formation of verbal sentence is very simple; for example: sometimes the same form of the verb is used for present and the past tenses. The word "ti" indicated a past tense or past participle.

Present tense	Past tense/Past Participle
Sùn - Sleep	Ti sùn, he/she has slept or he had slept
Jẹun - eat	Ti jeun, he/she has eaten or he had eaten
Lọ - go	Ti lọ, has gone or he had gone
Wi/sọ - say	So/wí - here the same form of the verb is used for present and the past tenses/past participle (e.g.) 1. Mo so fún lanan-I told him yesterday. 2. Olo àbí o kò lo lánăn - Did you go or not go yesterday?

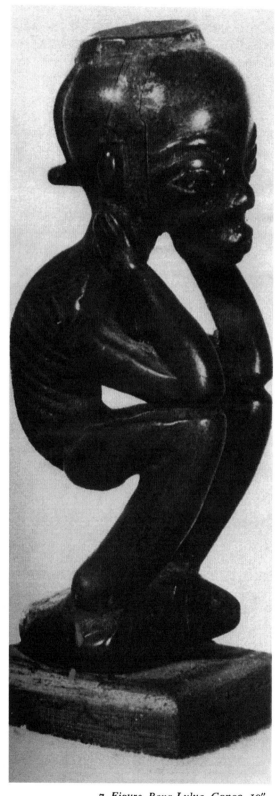

7. *Figure, Bena Lulua, Congo. 10"*

Again the word ti indicates both the perfect and the pluperfect, by placing the participle "ti" before the verb.

2. SUBSTANTIVE VERBS (verbs to be)

Yorùbá language has more than ten verbs that are expressing existence, there are verbs to be and most of them are verb absolute e.g.: ḿbe, wà, ya, sí, ri, ní, lí, gbé, dì, ṣe, and jé.

1. Ḿbe, Ọlọ́run. mbẹ - God exists, Màmá ḿbẹ nílé, mother is at home. Omin ḿbe lódò, there is water at the river.

2. Wà, is also a verb absolute, however, it is not entirely equivalent to ḿbe, existed (ó wà) (ḿbẹ) - he/she/it is there or exists, however, sometimes wà is preferred to ḿbẹ in modern Yorùbá conversation. Example: màmá/ńkó? How is mother? Wón wà, she is fine.

3. Ya - This verb is almost absolute also, the difference is that it is always used in negative abstract concept.

    Example: ya - change to, or become

    Ó ya odi - she/he became dumb

    Ó ya dindinrin - she/he became stupid

    Ó ya ìyàkuyà - she/he became wild

4. Sí This verb denotes existence in a place. Chiefly used in negative sentences as

    Example: Kò sí omi - there is no water

                Kò sí owó - there is no money

131 This mother with child by an Afo sculptor is among the finest treatments of the theme in the whole of Africa. It is thought to represent a female ancestor, the mother of the Afo people, for a similar piece is still in use in her shrine. The fact that the baby at her breast has herself mature breasts suggests that this is more than just an ordinary mother and child. Although few in numbers, the Afo enjoyed a high reputation as artists among neighbouring peoples, though their finest works seem to date from before 1900. Horniman Museum, London. Ht 27½ in.

Kò sí ounję - there is no food

Sé kò sí - hope there is nothing?

5.   Rí - This verb denotes a mode of existence, as in:

   1.   Báwo ló ti ri? How was it?

   2.   Bi a ti fę́ kó rí - The way we want it.

   3.   Bę̂ nâ ló rí - It was exactly so

 rí may also denote to see or seem to appear

6.   Ni/li whether used as a verb, pronoun, or preposition, usually

   comes before a vowel; for example:

   ní apa òtuń (or); lápá òtuń/on the right hand

   ní ębę́ ònà (or); légbę̀ ònà/by the road side

   ní ile (or); ni lé/at home

   ní ọ̀dọ̀ mọ̀mọ́: lọ́dọ̀ mọ̀mọ́/with mother

7.   Gbé - to dwell, reside, abide, live as in:

   1.   Nibo ni ęń gbé?/ Where do you live?

   2.   Òde ni ajá ágbé?/ A dog lives outside.

   3.   Èmi kò le gbé'bè./ I can not live there.

   4.   Nibo ló gbé?/ Where did he/she live?

   5.   Ta ló bá gbé?/ Who did she/he lived with?

8.   Di/ya, or di - to become, these three may be rendered by the verb to

   be, as in: Ọmọ mi di dókítà - my child has become a doctor.

   Omo nâ tiya ọmọ kómọ - the child has become bad/turn bad

175

YORUBA DRUM

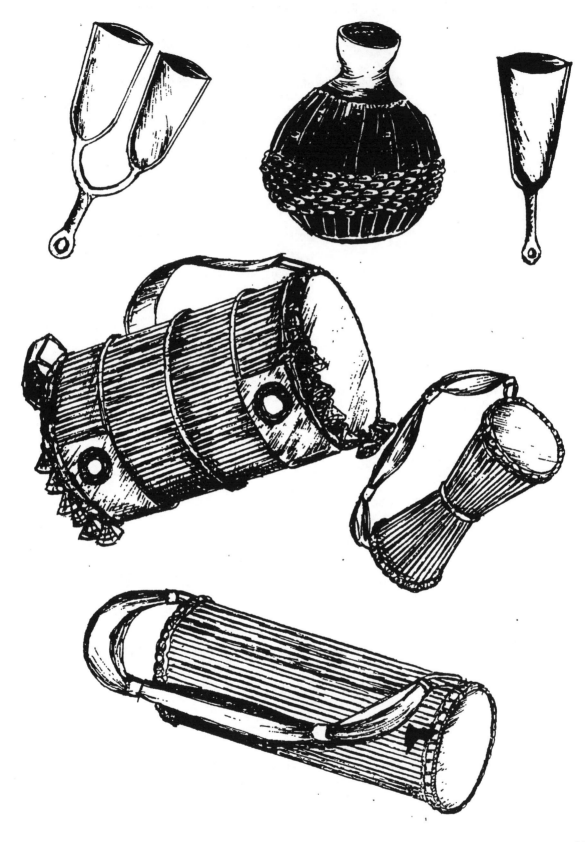

Any of the three verbs may be employed here

Bàbá ti di/da arúgbó or bàbá ti darúgbó - father has become old

Ó ti di/da àtúnbí or ó ti dàtúnbí - he/she is born again.

9. Se - The verb se, to do , to perform, to act or play may be rendered as a substantive in several cases as follows:

Nwọn se ojúse wọn - They played their part.

Yío se àmìn fun nyin - It will be a sign to you

Kín ni mo se? What did I do?

Èmi kò mo ẹni tíí se - I do not know who he/she is

Kìi se tìrẹ - it is not yours - here "se" expresses the relation of ownership.

10. Je - The verb "jé" is another form of "se" because the two verbs are very similar.

For example jé is expressed as follows:

Kín ni o jé - what capacity of an officer?

ninu'se ọlópà - what is your rank in the police force?

Kí ni o jé nínú ẹgbé - what is your office in the organization?

Tani o fi o je adájó - who made you a judge?

Jé is also the only word employed in the sense of "to be" with regard to numbers as in

Ó jé ogorum - it is one hundred

97 The Ata of Igala still wears the mask which Allen saw. It is called *Ejube auilo*, the eye which brings fear to other eyes, and is kept brightly polished. It is a Benin work of the late fifteenth or early sixteenth century, a period when there were substantial contacts between the two kingdoms. There are slits below the eyes which indicate that it was intended for wear over the face, a feature found on similar Benin masks in ivory and bronze. In this feature it may be compared with the Ife mask in *Ill. 40*. Property of the Ata of Igala, Idah. Ht 11½ in.

Also, in expressing refusal J<u>é</u> is employed as in èmi òjé lọ - I will

not go.

Ọlórun mo j<u>e</u> - God forbid

3. THE VERB "FE" AND "FERAN"

1. F<u>e</u> can mean want, like or love in English language, f<u>é</u> is one of

many meaningful monosyllabic verbs, other examples of such

verbs are:

2. In the case of the verb "f<u>é</u>" = love or like or want

"F<u>é</u>" can be used in sentences like these:

Mo f<u>é</u> omi - I want water

Mo f<u>é</u> jẹun - I want to eat

Mo f<u>é</u> ọsan - I want orange

The verb "f<u>é</u>ràn" is used when one is trying to express passion for

something.

Example:

1. Mo f<u>é</u>ràn re - I love you.

Mo "f<u>é</u>ràn" re t<u>ó</u>béég<u>é</u> - I love you very much

J<u>ù</u>, t<u>ó</u>béég<u>é</u> and p<u>ú</u>p<u>ò</u> mean - so much or very much

Ayò féràn owó j<u>ù</u> - Ayọ loves money too much (inform of criticism)

Mo féràn okò mi - I love my car

Mo féràn ọkò mi púpò - I so much love my car

Mo féràn ọkọ m<u></u> - I love my husband

Mo fẹ́ràn aya mi I love my wife

"Fẹ́ràn/Lati"

If you want to use another verb after "feran" you will need to use the word láti before the second verb and sometimes with pre-verb. (Maa) i.e. Tuńde fẹ́ràn láti máa kà'wé - Tuńde love to read.

Ọlá fẹ́ràn láti máa korin - Ola love to sing.

'Bọ́lá fẹ́ràn láti máa ràn sọ ᷉Bọ́lá love to sew.

Many times, we have to use monosyllabic verbs when talking about necessary desires, thus we do away with lati elision is always employed.

Examples:

Without elision	Mo fẹ́ mu omi	With elision Mo fe mu mi (I want water)
Without elision	Mo fẹ́ jẹ̀ ẹran	With elision Mo fẹ́ je ran (I want some meat)
Without elision	Mo fẹ́ lọsí Ilé	With elision Mo fẹ́ lọ le (I want to go home)
Without elision	Mo fẹ́ jẹ ouńje mi	With elision Mo fẹ́ jeun mi (I want to eat my food)

4.   LOCATIVE VERBS ("Ilé", Ibi, Ọ̀dọ̀) are locative nouns. You remember?

However, the locative verbs are underlined below.

Ọ̀dọ̀ tani o wà? Who have you been with?

Ọdọ tani ồun lo? Who are you going to?

"Ilé" simply means "house" but it is used many times as pre-noun. That is "ilé" can be used to refer to places of activities. Examples are:

1.   Mo ńlọ si ilé - I am going home. Here "ilé" is used a dwelling place.

2.   Mo ńlọ si ile ifowópamọ́ - I am going to the bank. Here "ile" is used as a pre-noun and a s a place of activity.

Similarly the Yoruba word "ibi" serves the same function as "ilé". You can either say: Ilé ijó = the bar

Examples:

1.   Mo ńlọ sí ilé ijó

I am going to the bar

2.   Mõ ńlọ sí ibi ijó

I am going to the bar

3.   Mõ ńlọ sí ibi iṣẹ́

I am going to work

Exercise:

Now construct your own five sentences using the locative verbs below and examples above. (i.e.) Ọdọ̀, ibi, ilé

1.   Construct five sentences with the word 'féràn' and 'fẹ́'

2.   List ten substantive verbs and employ each in a sentence.

3.   List ten Yoruba verbs and explain what each means.

#5 UNRESTRICTED PRE-VERBS

These pre-verbs do not exclude one another and the verbal particle go along with these pre-verbs some of them are:

1. "Ṣ̀èṣ̀è" - (have just) Mo ṣ̀èṣ̀è dé - I have just arrived.

2. "Jàjà" - (manage) Mo jàjà parí - I managed to finish.

3. "Kúkú" - (rather) Ma kúkú sùn - I rather sleep.

4. "Túbọ̀" - (further) Jọ̀wọ́ túbọ̀ sú_n - Please move further.

5. "Déédé" - (just) Ó déédé já búrẹ́dì gbà - He just snatched the bread.

6. "Tiẹ̀" - (even) – Nkò tiẹ̀ da lóhùn = I did not answer him.

7. "Sáá" - (however) - Mo sáá jẹun kín to kúro - however, I ate before leaving.

8. "Tún" - (again) - Mo tún pè léè kan ṣíì- I called him one more time.

9. "Mọ̀ọ́mọ̀ọ́" - (intentionally) - Mo mọ̀ọ́mọ̀ọ́ ṣe ni - I did it intentionally.

10. "Nìkan" - (by myself) Èmi nìkan ló jẹ tán - I finished the food by myself.

11. "Sábàá" - (usually) Dare sábàá ma nwale loso se - Dare come home weekly.

12. "Férèé" - (almost) Mo férèé pa ẹiyẹna) - He almost killed the bird.

13. "Fi" - (with) Kín lo fi nàá? - What did you beat him with?

14. "Ti" - (from) Níbo lo ti wá - Where did you come from?

15. "Da" - (alone) Ó dá se - He did it alone.

16. "Máa" - (continue) Máa bọ́rọ̀ rẹ nsó - Continue to speak.

17. "Kódà" - (even) Kódà ko wa - Even he did not come.

18. "Tèté" - (quickly) Jọ̀wọ́ tètè wa - Please come quickly.

19. "Sì" - (still) Mo sì tún nlọ sí ilé ìwé - I am still going to school.

20. "Lè" - (can) Mo lè rin - I can walk.

#6 AGREEMENT OF VERBS AND NOUNS

In Yorùbá, the verbs must agree with their nouns, which means that a singular verb and a plural verb.

EXAMPLES:

	SINGULAR	**PLURAL**
1.	Ọmọ ná ńkọrin sókè. The boy sings loudly.	Àwọn ọmọ nâ ńkọrin sókè. The boys sing loudly.
2.	Ajá ńgbó lókè odò. The dog barks over the river.	Awọn ajá ńgbó lókè odò. The dogs bark over the river.
3.	Ọmọ ̃mi ńkọrin. My child sings.	Àwọn ọmọ mi ńkọrin. My children sing.

In English, a noun ending in 's' is often a plural, whereas a verb ending in 's' is usually singualar, i.e. runs in paint, he runs the errand (singular verb). However, this is not the case in Yoruba language. The word "awọn" readily distinguishes plural forms.

#7 Construction of Sentences using the <u>first person pronouns</u> plus a <u>verb</u> and a <u>noun</u>.

- Mo fẹ́ àga kan - I want a chair.

- Mo fẹ́ omi díê - I want some water.

- Mo fẹ́ dùrù kan - I want an organ.

- Mo fẹ́ ewé kan - I want a leaf.

- Mo fẹ́ èpà díe - I want some peanuts (ground-nuts).

- Mo fẹ́ fìlà kan - I want a cap.

- Mo fẹ́ garawa kan - I want a pail.

183

- Mo fẹ́ gbòǹgbò kan - I want a root.

- Mo fẹ́ ehín díẹ̀ - I want some teeth.

- Mo fẹ́ ìwé kan - I want a book.

- Mo fẹ́ jigí kan - I want a mirror.

- Mo fẹ́ kẹ̀kẹ́ kan - I want a bicycle.

- Mo fẹ́ labalábá kan - I want a butterfly.

- Mo fẹ́ màalũ kan - I want a cow.

- Mo fẹ́ lọ si Nigeria - I want to visit Nigeria..

- Mo fẹ́ ọ̀gẹ̀dẹ̀ díẹ̀ - I want some bananas.

- Mo fẹ́ bàtà pupa - I want a red shoe.

- Mo fẹ́ ràkúnmí kan - I want a camel.

- Mo fẹ́ sálúbàtà kan - I want a sandal.

- Mo fẹ́ sòkòtò kan - I want a pair of pant/trouser.

- Mo fẹ́ tòlótòló kan - I want a turkey.

Exercise: Now construct ten sentences using the first person pronouns plus a verb

and noun as demonstrated above, then underline the verbs and circle the nouns.

NEGATORS

There are four negators in Yorùbá.

(a) Kò (b) O (c) Ki (d) Ma, Both Ko and Q can occur before and after a verb.

(a). (1) "Kò", Bàbá so pé kò sí owó. - Father said there is no money.

- Bólá mọ̀ pé kò sí omi mọ́. - Bọla knew there is no more water.

- Àwìn kò sí lóni. - There is no credit today.

184

(b). (1) "Ò" ẹ ọ̀ muu. - You can not catch it.

2. ẹ ọ̀ lè lọ. - You can not go.

3. ẹ ọ̀ lè mọ̀ - You can not tell or say.

(c). (1) Kíi or Kò Kíi ṣiṣẹ́ - (Combinations of negators). He doesn't work.

2. Kò jẹ bẹ̀ni kò mu - he/she/neither ate nor drank

3. Kì bá má gbà - he/she must not fail to come.

4. Kò kíi sùn bẹ̀ni kíi tòògbé/He neither sleep nor slumber.

Kò gbọdọ̀ má lọ - he/she would not have gone.

(d). (1) Kì bá má lọ - he/she would not have gone.

2. Kò gbọdọ̀ má lọ - He/she must not fail to go.

3. Kògbọdọ̀ má -ṣeé - he must not fail to do it.

Exercise: Construct six negators using the four Yorùbá negators "kò", "ò", "kíi", and "má" at least two from each negator.

More Practice on Elision

Without Elision	With Elision	English
Sé alaafià ni?	Sálaafia ni ?	Is it peaceful with you? (or) Are you o.k.?
Níbo ni o ti wá?	Nibó loo tiwá?	Where have you been?
Nibo ni ẹ̀ ńlọ?	Níbo lẹ̀ ńlọ ?	Where are you going?
Ta ni on lu ìlù?	Ta lón lù'lù ?	Who is drumming?
Kí ni o ti wí	Kí lo ti wí ?	What did you say?
Kí ni orúkọ rẹ	Kí lo rúko rẹ ?	What is your name?
Kí ni Ònṣe	Kí lò ńṣe ?	What are you doing?
Bí o bá fẹ́	Bó bá fẹ́ ?	If you want.

185

Di ojú re	Dijú re	Close your eyes.
Dá èrù bà ó	Dérù bà ó	Scared you.
Ní òla	Lola	Tomorrow.
Ó jà mí ní olè	Ójà mí ló lè	He/she stole my properties.
Mo bá olómo yò	Mo bólómo yò	I rejoice with new parents.
Mo ríe ní Ilé ejó	Mo ríe nílé ejó	I saw you in the court house.
Fi aso bo omo ná	Faso b'omo náà	Cover the baby with cloth.
Fi sílè jé kó lo	Fií lè jé ólo	Leave him/her, let him/her go

Exercise: List ten examples of Yoruba words without elision and write elision of the words listed.

#10 The Use of Verbal Groups

The Yoruba verbal root remains unchanged through out all the variations of person, number, mode, and tense. Persons and number are devoted by the form of the personal pronoun that represents the subjects. The following examples denotes the verb group, that is a <u>word or group</u> of words which can stand as predicate of a clause, or a verbal group.

Example 1: Predicate of a clause

"Ìbá or Kìbá" - (he or she or it) would have.

"Kíi" - kíi sun - (he or she or it) does not sleep.

"Máa" - máá lo lóla - I will go tomorrow.

"Yòo" - èmi yo lo pèlu nwon - I will go with them.

Gbòdo - Ko gbodò lo - he must not go.

"A" - bóyá a lo - watch and see if (he/she/it) will go.

Example 2:

Plural	Singular of Predicate of a Clause
Èmí lo - I went	Àwá lo - we went
Ì wó lo - you went	Èyín lo - Ye went or you went
Ó lo - He went	Nwon lo - They went

#11 Types of Verbs

There are three types of verbs: The preverbs, the free verbs and the post verbs.

1.   The pre-verbs are followed by another verb whenever they occur in verbal

   groups, and they are called the pre-verbs, they consist of verbal particles.

Example 3: "ti" pre-verb

Mo ti setán - I have finished.

Mo ti de - I have come.

Mo ti jeun - I have eaten.

2.   The free-verbs are those particles that can occur independently in the verbal

   group.

Example 4:

   •   Ó ní - He said

   •   Ó wá - he came

   •   Ó rí - he/she saw

   •   Ó ké - he/she shouted

187

- Ó fẹ́ - he/she wants

- Ó dé - he arrived

- Ó pẹ́ - he was late

Example 5:

Mo lọ sí ojà - I went to the market.

Mo lọ sí ilé ìwé - I went to school.

Mo lọ sí odò - I went to the river.

Mo lọ sí sósì - I went to church.

The pre-verbs are: verbal particle, restricted pre-verbs, unrestricted pre-verbs, and negators.

1. The verbal particle, that is, the particle of continuance, such as "n" or "m".

2. The particle "n" sometimes exchange for "m" before "b", is probably a contraction of "ni" to be examples on the use of "n" particle.

'n' ńlá - to be great	➡	Mo ní ayọ̀ ńlá - I have great joy
'n' ńlọ - to be going	➡	Nwọn tiń lọ - they are going
'n' njẹun - to be eating	➡	Bàbá njẹun lọ́wọ́ - Bàbá is eating
'n' ńfọ̀ - to be washing	➡	Mọmọ́ ńfọ aṣọ - Mọmọ is washing
'n' sùn - to be sleeping	➡	Ọmọ ńâ ńsùn lọ́wọ́ - the baby is sleeping

The 'm' particle is used as follows:

Nwọ́n ti mbọ̀ - they are coming.

Ó ti mbá wagbé - He's been living with us.

Nwón mbá wa rin - They are walking with us.

1. The use of 'n' or 'm' conjugation is to denote a continuing or unfinished (present continuous tense).

    Ọmọ ńsùn - the child is sleeping

    Nígbàti àwa mbọ̀ láti ọjà lánǎn - When we were coming from the market yesterday.

2. The restricted pre-verbs. The pre-verbs generally exclude excess verbal particle. Bá - to meet or arrive at, it is employed as an auxiliary particle. Chiefly in what may be termed the subjuacture mode.

    Exercise

    a. List three types of verbs.
    b. Employ each of these verbs in three sentences.
    c. What is verbal particle?
    d. Construct five sentences each with particles "n", "m" and "ba".

(i.e.) • mo bá e jó - I dance with you.
        • mo bá e yò - I rejoice with you.
        • Màá bá e lọ - I will go with you.
        • Mo bá ẹ - I catch up with you.

A typical nuclear Yorùbá family is composed of the grandparents, called "bàbá mi àgbà" and Mòmó àgbà by ground their children, Father "bàbá mi" and Mother, "mòmó mi," their immediate children, the uncles, nieces, and the cousins from both sides. The Yorùbás really value sense of unity, for this reason, the word "cousin" or "niece" or "uncle"do not exist in their vocabularies. If you are a related man, you will either be addressed as father "bàbá mi" or brother. Likewise, if you are a related woman, you will either be addressed mother, màmá mi or sister "ègbón mi".

The Yorùbás are so possessive of their family members, you will notice when a child addresses his or her father, they say "bàbá mi" / my father or "màmá mi"/my mother or mom as its the case in the West. Family bond is very evident and strong in Yorùbá land, and the phases, "Okùn omo yà yí"/the rope that ties family together is very strong or "blood is thicker than water"/èjè ki ju omi lo" these phrases have deep meanings to the Yorùbá people.

In the Yorùbá culture, women are usually known by the name of their firstborn child. So, most people would call a mother "màmá-Bùmi" or Mòmó Dayo. In many culture, for a variety of reasons, a child is named on the 8th day (the birth-day is the 1st day, so the 8th day is exactly a week later) of their life. A whole 'naming ceremony' usually accompany this.

Though this is also changing, most men are raised with the expectation that someday they will have a wife (or wives) to take care of them, and most women are raised with the expectation that someday they will have a husband and children to take care of. So, the standards for raising them can differ in some households. In most neighborhoods, the neighbors take a part in taking care of a child. A lot of people feel like they were raised by the neighborhood because "it takes a whole village to raise a child." Hillary Radom Clinton, 1996.

MARRIAGE CEREMONY IN THE YORÙBÁ CULTURE TODAY

Most modern day weddings in Nigeria today are resembling the Western wedding procedures. More and more wedding programs are held in the churches and courts of law. The churches and courts law, only a few wedding programs in the Yoruba land today are completely traditional.

THE INTRODUCTION

This is the part of the ceremony where the groom's family introduces themselves to the bride's family, and asks for their daughter's hand in marriage to their son. It would take place before the engagement ceremony or wedding. The participants are:

- The groom and his family

- **Olópǎ Ìduro** (this translates to 'standing policeman'): an appointed speaker by the groom's family; could be a family member, or hired for the occasion.

- The bride and her family

- **Olópǎ Ìjókǒ** (this translates to 'sitting policeman'): an appointed speaker by the bride's family; could be a family member, or hired for the occasion.

- Others if the families so choose.

The introduction takes place at the bride's house, and her family is responsible for the preparations and costs, but if the groom's family is able to, they can suggest helping out with some of the costs of the program. "African time" is common in Nigeria , however , the groom's family is expected to be on time for this event. If they are late, the bride's family may ask them to leave, or to pay a price for being late. Upon entrance into the bride's home, the groom's family kneels (the women do that) or prostrate (the men do that) for the bride's parents. The groom's family and the bride's family sit on opposite sides of the room, with the bride and the groom sitting closer to the center, and the olópǎ idúró and olópǎ ìjokǒ sitting in the very middle. The olópǎ idúró introduces the groom and his family to the bride and her family. He then brings a proposal letter from the groom's family, through the olópǎ ìjókǒ. The letter is read out and responded verbally on the spot. Since this is mostly a formality, and it is already known that the couple will marry, usually rejection is unexpected at this point. It is still customarily important for the groom's family to provide the bride's family with dowry (owó-ori-íyàwó) that would go to the bride's parents to compensate for some of the costs of raising her. However, today if a dowry is offered, it usually goes directly to the bride. Prayer are offered this point, and some symbolic items of food are tasted by the olópǎ's and then passed around to the guests. These include:

- Obì (kola nut) is shared, during which the following words are repeated.

  Wọ́n má gbó (they will ripe)(They would be couple)

  Wọ́n má tọ́ (they will eat and not go hungry)

  Wọn ma d'agba (they will grow old)

- Ata ire (aligator peper): this consists of many seeds, and it is opened up, and the superstition is that the number of seeds that fall out is the number of children the couple will bear. (Ata ire ki di tirẹ̀ láabọ) aligator peper is full of seeds, the same they wish for the couple.

- Oyin (honey), sugar ireke (sugar cane): these all symbolize that the union will be sweet.

Some additional words may be exchanged, gifts are exchanged then the families and guests eat traditional food, and there may be singers and drummers for the celebration later.

THE ENGAGEMENT

Sometimes the engagement ceremony takes place right after the Introduction. Traditionally, a couple is married after the engagement ceremony. There has to be a legal registration of the couple. The engagement ceremony also takes place at the bride's house, and her family is once again responsible for that. Both parties are dressed in **aso** òkè, the is more fanciful and more expensive Nigerian attire. The symbolic food may be passed around again. The couple usually gives each other a Bible or Quran, they exchange gift of rings, and they may say some words to each other.

Ìyàwó de ile ọkọ rẹ

The bride has got to her new husband's home; her feet must be washed.

The bride usually has her face covered during the ceremony. When the ceremony is over, and everyone had left. She will wait indoor until she is called out by her parents. Then she comes out (usually with a friend, still with her face covered), and kneels before her parents so that they may pray for her. She kneels before the groom's parents also, so that she can receive their blessing too. Then she sits by the groom, and this is when she is unveiled, as she sits to eat with everybody. Along with the food, there is usually a cade in the shape of a Bible or Quran. After the couple is married, they go to the groom's house (his house, not necessarily his family's house). The custom is that the bride should arrive at his home before he does, and that she must wash her legs before entering, and be there to meet him when he arrives. Customs that used to take place in some Nigerian cultures are:

- The bride-to-be was kept in a 'fattening room' for a period of time, where she was well fed, and taught how to be a good wife. She usually came out of the room fatter than before.

- The bride-to-be was 'cleansed' by taking a special bath before going to her husband.

- Right after the wedding ceremony, the bride has her feet washed so that she may get to her husband clean.

- Rather than bringing out the real bride at the engagement party, another woman may come out disguised as the bride to see if the groom is able to tell the difference.

MARRIAGE TIDBITS

The following are facts/trends in the marriage structure. Though traditionally, both parties were supposed to be virgins on the wedding night (unless it is not the groom's first marriage of course), at least in the Yorùbá culture, it is common nowadays for the bride to be pregnant before the wedding because the couple wants to ensure that they can have children (this is not allowed in Christian marriage, because abstinence from sexual activities is expected of a Christian.

- Polygamy is legal for the male in Nigeria
  - ... but not in the Christian religion.
  - In traditional beliefs, a man is allowed to have unlimited number of wives.
  - In the Muslim religion, it is legal for a man to have up to 4 wives at one time.
  - The first wife is supposed to have more respectable status, but the most recent wife is usually considered the 'favorite of the husband.'
- Though it is legal, polygamy is becoming less common for economic reasons, thus polygamous life seems unaffordable.
- In polygamous households, the man is supposed to be financially responsible for the family.
- In most households and most religions, the man is the head of the household.
- Arranged marriages used to be more common in terms of an arbitrator looking for a spouse for a young man or woman.

- In some cultures, arranged marriages in terms of children being promised in marriage at young ages were also common.

FATHER'S ROLE HAS NO SUBSTITUTE

NEWLY WEDS

When a Baby Is Born

When a new baby is born in Yorùbá land, both the family of the wife will come around to congratulate the new mother and the new father. They will say "Báríkà! Báríkà!! Ekú ewu ọmọ, adúpẹ́ tiá gbọ́ ohùn ìyá, ti'a sì tuń gbọ́ ohun ọmọ." This means congratulations! We are grateful to hear the voice of the mother and the voice of the child. They are simply congratulating the family because the child and the mother survived the agony of labor.

In order to know the sex of the baby, people ask several questions like "akọ ni tàbi abo?" "Is it a he or a she?" "A husband or a wife?" "Ọkọ ni tàbi 'yawo?" "The owner of the house or a guest?" "Onílé ni tàbi àlejò?" "Irú tèmi ni tàbi tirẹ?" "Does the baby look like me "a guy" or like you "a lady?"

Yorùbá names are given according to the circumstances obtained in a respective family at birth of a child. Hence, the Yorùbás say, Ilé làá wò ká tó ó ṣọmọ lórúko, that is the circumstances in a family is considered before naming a child. Other proverbs that emphasize the importance of "name" in Yoruba land are, "Orúkọ ẹni ijánu ẹni," that is, name is the source of conscious awareness or the grand mother of the conscience. The Yorùbá believe that name is fragile, once it is damaged, it will be almost impossible to redeem. Another one is "Orúkọ ńro ni" that means, a name can really motivate or prompt a person, for example, the Yorùbás also say that ọmọ ti yío ba jẹ Asamu, láti kékeré ni ti ti jẹnu sámú sámúulọ. This means that most of the time, name reflects character. All these emphasize the importance of name in Yorùbá land.

The Yorùbás start to think about what name the baby will bear immediately the pregnant woman goes into labor.

TYPES OF NAMES

1. Orúkọ àbiso – Christened names

2. Orúkọ àbíkú – names of children that come and go

3. Orúkọ oríkì – the family praise names

4. Orúko amuntorun wa – names brought from heaven

5. Orúkọ àjèjì – foreign names

6. Orúkọ àníjé or ìnagije – nicknames

7. Orúkọ oyè and oruko adape – chieftaincy names

The Àbíso Names – Orúkọ Àbíso

The orúkọ àbíso which can be roughly translated as "christened" names usually consists of many components, and consequently long in many cases. These components can contain other short or shortened names in category of àbíso. It also shows the type of family a child is born into. Some examples of àbíso names include the following: 1. Royal Family names that begin with or end with words of prefix-names like:

Adé-crown, Adé-yẹmí-the crown befits me

Adé-lọwọ-the crown commands honor and respect

Adéléké-The triumphant prince

Adéwùmí-Crown is my passion

Adéoyè-The crown is the symbol of royalty

Adékúnlé-Ours is the family of royalty

Adéwunyi-The cherishable and popular prince

Adégbàmíké-A treasured prince

Adédayò-The victorious prince

Adédiran-I am the heir of royalty

Adéwálé-The prince is back home

Títíladé-The crown is mine forever

Oyè (title or chieflancy),   Oyèdéle – We are of royal family

                                  Oyèwùmí – Royalty is my passion

                                  Oyègbémidé – I was born royal

                                  Oyèkólá – Royalty attracts wealth

                                  Oyèmákin – Royalty is connected with heroism

                                  Títíloyè – Royalty for life

Olú (Lord or authority),   Olúlówò – The Lord commands reverence

                                  Olúdárà – The Lord is full of wonders

                                  Olúdáre – The Lord justifies

                                  Olúségun – The Lord is victorious

                                  Olúbisí – The Lord multiplies

Olá - (Affluence, treasure or nobility for example)

Olánrewájú – My success is ever progressive

Ọláwálé – The treasured one is back home

Ọlá Olú – The wealth is of the Lord

The Yorùbá people of the warriors family, or those who are responsible for the protection of life and properties, bear names with affixable components like:

Ògún (war) i.e.   Abógundé – Born during war or wars

                    Ògúngbémidé – War had brought me here

                    Ògúngbèmí – I benefitted from the war

                    Adúrógbangba – A courageous individual

                    Igi Ogun – A warlike individual

                    Fijàbí – Born when there was war

                    Abíógun – Born into war

                    Adógundádé – The war had brought about the crown

Akin (A man of valor or a hero, such as):

                    Akínwándé – I am fully heroic

                    Akinadé – I am a person of royalty and hero

                    Akíndélé – The man of valor is now home

                    Akínwùmí – I desire to be a hero

                    Akínnúbi – I am of the family of hero

Èsọ́ (Protection, custody or security, guarded and treasured people)

Èsọ́wùmí – I am a desired treasure

Èsọ́gbémiró – I am a secured treasure

Èsọ́diran – The heirs of treasure

Ẹ̀sódàyísí – I am a spared treasure

Ẹ̀sọ́kúnlé – The family of guarded treasure

Ẹ̀sọ́rìnọ́lá – This treasure is an afluent

Ẹ̀sọ́dọlá – This treasure is the source of wealth

Àyàn (drummers' diety) signifies the descendants of drummers and signers, some musicians or entertainers. Examples are:

Àyánrìnọ́lá – An affluent drummer

Àyànlolá – There is wealth in drumming

Àyánkólá – Entertaining attracts wealth

Àyángbèmí – Drumming really pays

Àyándélé – The success of music is brought home

Ọnà (god of art and creativity) the worshipers of the diet bear name that mostly begin or end with these deities. The names are related to Yorùbá cavers, sculptors, painters, and traditional craft works. Some examples of those are:

Ọnǎyẹmí – Craftsmanship befits me

Ọnàladé – A successful craft worker

Ọnàgbèmí – I benefit from carving

Ọnǎrìndé – A successful craft person is here

Similarly, names containing Ifá (i.e.) Ifagbemi, – Ifá is the source of my success.

Ifájọbí – From Ifa all of us are born

Ifádáre – Ifa had justified me

Ifákúnlé – Our home is full of Ifa worshipers

Ifánίyì – Ifá is very desirable

Ifáwùmί – I desire to worship Ifá

Ifádìran – I am a heir of Ifá

Ifáwọlé – Ifá is back home

Ifágbèmί – Ifá benefits me a lot

Ifáyẹmί – I benefit from Ifá/Ifá benefits me

Ifábáyọ̀ – Ifá had met with joy in me

Ifádípè – Ifá pleads to all the bad spirits

Signifies the family of the Ifá diety worshipers. Other Ifá diety worshiper's names (i.e.) Odù – divinity (Odù Ifá) = Ifá divinity.

Odù,   Odùdárà – The divinity is the source of wonders

Oduòlá – The divinity brings about wealth

Odùgbèmί – I triumph from the divinity

Oduỳẹmί – The divinity befits me

Odùduwà – The divinity that gave birth to good character.
(Odù tó bί ìwà)

Awo – diety   Awolówò – There is honor in worshipping Awo

Awódìran – I am heir of Awo

Awóyẹmί – Awo befits me

Awódáre – Awo justifies me

Awodárà – Awo performs wonder

Sàngó, (god of thunder and lightning)

Ṣàngólàdé – Ṣàngó had me succeeded

Ṣàngódélé – Ṣàngó had brought success home

Ṣàngógbèmi – Ṣàngó had made me proud

Ṣàngóléke̖ – Ṣàngó had made me triumph

Ògún, (god of iron)   Ògúnlàdé – Ògún had made me successful

Ògúndáre – Ògún had justified me

Ògúnyẹmí/Ògúngbèmí – I benefit a lot from worshipping Ògún

Ògúnsèyí – Ògún had done this

Ògúndìran – I am a heir of Ògún

It is necessary to note that Àbíso names now abound in their variety among the Yorùbá elite. Some of these names are persuasively full of positive fantasy; they are also imaginative and meaningful.

Examples:

Abíso Names for Females	Abíso Names for Males
Títílayọ–My Joy is Everlasting	Adédayọ̀–Triumphant prince (male or female
Ayọ̀bámi–Joy is mine always	Olújídé–Rise again
Olúfúnmiké–God has given you to me to adore	Kóláwọlé–Wealth is brought home by me
Àduké–The widely esteemed child	Olúfémi–God loves me
Olútóyìn–God is worthy of praises	Olúségun–Victory from God (God is victorious)
Olúkẹ́mi–God has satisfied me	Olúdáre–God justifies

Female Names	Male Names
Olúbùnmi–A surprise gift from God	Olúbùkáyò–God has added to joy
Olúwáseun–God is full of goodness	Olúgbémiga–God elevates me
Olúfúnmiláyò–The Lord has given me joy	Kólapò–Make the wealth plentiful
Olúrèmí–The Lord has comforted me	Adépéjú–All the heirs are here
Olúsadé–The Lord has provided me with His crown	Adéníran–Crown is in my heritage
Olúyémisí–The Lord has honored me	Adéwàle–The prince is back home

THE ÀBÍKÚ NAMES – ORÚKỌ ÀBÍKÚ

Àbíkú means "born to die" this is the Yorubas label for the children who are believed to possess a nauseating spirit that afford them to enter mother's wombs. They die soon after delivery for no apparent reasons or born and die mostly before they turn ten years old. The "àbíkú names" usually show the passion and fantasy of the 'abíkús' parents, hence they sound protective, pleading and sometimes commanding.

Examples of these names are:

Ikúshmò – Death has failed to recognize this baby

Ikúmópàyí – Death please don't kill this one

Ikúforíjì – Death had forgiven us

Ikúdaisí– Death has spared this for us

Àmòsá – Boringly or We are tired of you "come and go"

Kòsókó – there's no hoe to dig ground for anymore burials

Ọkọya – The hoe is damaged

Dúrówojú – Live (baby) in order for you to enjoy my company

Dúrósinmí – Live in order for you to survive or bury me (your parent)

Dúrójayé – Live so that you too can enjoy life

DúrósingJésù – Live so you can serve the Lord Jesus

Orúko Oríkì

Parents and elderly Yorùbá use oriki names to praise their children, to pay tribute to an affluent person, to entreat, or appease the kings and queens. Oríkì names can motivate and persuade the person being praised to perform better either while dancing, wrestling, or while spending money. Oríkì names are influenced by fantasy employed by mothers and grandmothers to encourage their children. Oríkì names are also used by praise singers, e.g., musicians and drummers to exalt the chiefs, the kings and to invoke their spirit and that of their ancestors.

Examples of the male and female oriki names are as follows:

Male Oríkì Names	Female Oríkì Names
Àdigún	Àbèbí
Àdìò	Àbèó
Àdìsá	Àdùké
Àjàgbé	Àdùnní
Àjaní	Àmòké
Àjao	Àlàké
Àjàlá	Àsàbí
Àlàgbé	Àṣelé
Àkanbí	Awẹní
Àkàngbé	Àweró
Àkàbì	Àtóké
Àsàmú	Àyìnké
Àyìnlá	Àsaké
Àrèmú	Àsùnké
Àlào	Òdèré
Àkànbí	Àbèní
Àjào	Àríké
Àlàdé	Àbẹgbé
Àkàngbé	

207

Names brought from heaven (Orúko Àmútòrunwá)

These are natural names that explain the physical condition of the baby at delivery and its hierarchy in the sequence of siblings. The following are some names in the amutorunwa category, most of them are unisex.

Táiwò or Táyé (Tó aiyé wò) is the name of the first born of a pair of twins (ìbejì)

Kéhìndé or Akéhìndé gbègbón (The last to arrive but takes the seniority among the twins.

Èta (or) Èta Òkò is the name given to the third child of the triplets while the first two are named like the pair of twins.

Idòwú is the name of the child born after a pair of twins by the same mother or the first two are named like the pair of twins.

Àlàbá is the name of the child born after Idowu.

Ọla is the name of the child born after alaba.

Ọtunla is the name of the child born after Ola.

Edùn is the name of twin.

Òní is the child who cries a lot immediately after birth and thereafter.

Ìgè is the name of the child who was born with legs in front instead of head.

Àjàyí is the name of the child born in breech position (with face down).

Ìlòrí is the name of the child born when mother did not have menstrual period.

Àìná is the name of the female child born with umbilical cord around her neck.

<u>Òjó</u> is the name of the male child born with umbilical cord around her neck.

<u>Òké</u> is the child born with unbroken "bag of water."

<u>Dàda</u> is the child born with dreadlocks and plenty of hair, cries when it is combed.

<u>Talàbí</u> is the name of the child born with torn membrane.

<u>Olúgbódi</u> is the name of the child born with six fingers.

<u>Family Circumstantial Names</u>

Other names that can also be "àbíso" but also fit into this category are:

<u>Dáwódù</u> is the first male child.

<u>Bèèrè</u> is the first female child.

<u>Òkánlàwón</u> is the name of the male child born after many females.

<u>Morénıkéjì</u> is called the second female child born after many males born after the first female.

<u>Abíónà</u> is the name of the child given birth on a journey.

<u>Yétúndé</u> is the female child born after the death of a grandmother or mother.

<u>Abídèmí</u> is any child (unisex) born before the father came back from long terminal journey (i.e.) overseas.

<u>Babátúndé</u> 'jídé, 'rìndé, 'dèhìndé is the male child born after the death of a grandfather, senior or old respectable man in a family.

<u>Tòkunbò</u> is the child born while it rained, or a child born overseas before being brought to the homeland.

Abíọdún or Bọ́dúndé is the child born during a festival (i.e.) Christmas.

THE FOREIGN NAMES (ORÚKỌ ÀJÈJÌ)

In the category of foreign names, we have those names adopted from religions like Christianity, Islam, Hindu, etc., and those that were suppressively given to the Yoruba descendants who were barbarously forced away as slaves. These names, are called by the late Afro-beat Star, Fela just as "slave name." It is worthwhile to mention here that almost every Yorùbá family nowadays, tend to give their children these foreign names, especially religious names, which most Yorùbá children eventually maintain, reject or suppress when they grow up. Unfortunately, these foreign names have supplanted the status of the 'abiso' names among the Yorùbá.

Such means are easy to detect, in that most of them, in the first instance, are disobedient to Yorùbá orthographic principles that disallow consonant clusters. Secondly, they contain consonants that are not available in Yorùbá alphabets. Many of these are renown family names in Nigeria generally and they are sometimes combined with Yorùbá names via hyphen where by the first or the second part of the names are either Yorùbá or foreign ones. Names like Ranson-Kúti, Okóya-Thomas, Williams, Benson, Thompson, Johnson, Braithwaite, Nagregor, Bucknor, Craig, Adomson, Arinson, Coker, Badmos, Ezekiel, Rachel, Esther, Jimoh, Mohammed, Ahemed, Rasheed, Bashir, etc., are good examples of (Orúko-Àjèjì), foreign names.

THE NICKNAMES (ORÚKỌ INAGIJE OR ANÌJẸ)

Àníjẹ́ or Ìnagije is a nickname. Another type of name that will be discussed comprehensively below and that fits well into this category is Orúko-Ìyàwó.

(1).   The Orúkọ Ànìjẹ́ category, there are names manufactured by groups, comrades or by oneself and by wives in the Yorùbá families. The names explain the disposition, competence or feat of a person. They can be metaphorical, flattering and short of explanatory and long. Anije is used among friends and comrades or in the family in the case of Orúkọ-Ìyàwó. No family members call their ward these names. Close relations, friends and age, play or schoolmates only know of, and use these names and they are not given or answered officially by the Yorùbá unlike, Àbísọ, Oríkì, Àmútòrunwá and Oyè. Examples of these names are: Ẹkùn (tiger=aggressive and powerful), Bàlógunlẹ́hìn obìnrin (womansier or flirt), Ìjàpá (tortoise=stingy and or shrewd), Igbin (Snail=slow and wise) etc. It is necessary to mention that it is very common nowadays among the Yoruba youth to shorten or coin fashionably either by themselves or their friends.

Examples are following nicknames: Show from names beginning with Sho, Adey from bò láji, Solly from -solá, Dolly from -dọla, Lolly from ²Lọla, Jajel from Jajekodunmi, Fakus from Fákúnmọjù, Lad from-Ladipo, Tai from Táíwò or Táyẹ́, Kẹmo from -kẹ́mi, etc. In this trend, initials of names are also created by adopting the two alphabet at the initial position, or one at the beginning, and the second from the middle or the end of names. Examples of these are: ID created from Idowu, Ig. From Ìgè, TJ. From Túnjí, Bb. From Bímbọ́, etc.

(2.)   **ORUKỌ ÀDÀPÈ BY THE NEW WIVES**

Orúkọ-Ìyàwó explains names given to children by new wives in Yorùbá family. They are pet, characteristic (physical and behavioral), flattering or critical

211

names invented by the new Yorùbá wives for their young in-laws. The young nice, neat, brilliant, gentle, etc., in-laws are given fine and adorable names while the stubborn, nagging, rude or disobedient ones in the family are conferred critical or personified names.

Members of the family junior to a bearer of such names usually adopt same and join the wives in calling the names temporarily (until they grow up) since Yorùbá culture do not simply call elderly people or their seniors (whether by age or status) by name. It is worth diverting a bit and explain that "a Yorùbá" is customarily compelled to add something to the names and sometimes nicknames of such people. Children of the honorary names, same biological parents are expected to respect each other in accordance with the hierarchy of their birth.

When they become mature they automatically change to accept standard of addressing the elderly ones by adding "Ẹ̀gbọ́n mi" (elderly-my elder/senior) before calling the names of or referring to their elder brothers, sisters and the other next of kin. "Nowadays they sometimes use Bòùdá or Aḣuti mi (my brother or sister) instead of "Ẹ̀gbọ́n" or "Bòùdá" before calling the person's real name to indicate that they are closely related.

In as much as most wives are expectedly older than these young in-laws or equal in age, and it is against the Yorùbá culture to simply call an elderly person by names, it thus becomes reasonable and justified to show respect to wives by calling them "iyawo" (wife) and they reciprocate with the invented names below. It needs to be stressed that many of these wives also look after and sometimes train these

212

young in-laws. Some of the names like Ọmọ-jéjé (gentle kid), Adúmáadán or Máradán (Black and Shine), ọmọ ilé-ìwé (school kid), Aselébé (one who is thin and flexible), Ọmọdúdú (extra dark complexion child), Ọmọpupa (child with fair complexion) are fine unisex names. Some male names of this sort are Ajísafé (one who likes enjoyment and dodges responsibilities). Admirable female names are ibadi-aran (beautiful girl with befitting hip for beads), Afínjú (fastidious girl), Ehín-afé (girl with fine structured teeth), Ehínfúnjowó (girl with beautiful white teeth), Ẹléyinjúẹgé or Ẹyinjúẹgé (girl with beautiful or delicate eyes), Apónbéporé (fair complexion and beautiful girl), Ọpéléngé (slender and beautiful girl) etc., Arómimáwè (dirty child, Onígbe (crying child) among others, are corrective critical names.

ORÚKO OYÈ-CHIEFTANCY TITLE NAMES

Orúko Oyè defines traditional or chieftancy title assumed by or conferred onto one. Some of these are assumed or conferred hereditarily, while others are meritoriously or hierachiacally attained. The heredity ones are the crown or throne names of the Yorùbá soverigns, emissaries, priests, etc. Names like Ọni, Aláàfin, Aláké, Àtáója, Oíle, Àgùrà, Olówu, Olúbara, Olúbàdàn, Awùjalè, Olúwǒ Akilè, Olú, Àtáója, Esunmòwé, Sǫún, Aláyé, Ọlǫ̀fin, Alárá Ajérò, Ọràngún, Olóri, Ayinba, etc.

MERITORIOUSLY ATTAINED TITLE NAMES

Meritoriously attained title names are Basọrun, Ọtún, Òsi, Alárẹ, Akógun, Balógun, Jagunmólú, Ɛrẹlú, Ìyálodé, etc., and a typical example of a royal title is that hierachically attained in Yorùbáland is Olúbàdàn. Some of these names, like

213

Balógun, Asiwájú, Olówu, Jagun, Basòrun, etc., have establishingly become proper family names in Yorùbáland.

Conclusively, the following is a brief analysis of the names of the Nigerian Nobel laureate for literature, Professor Wolé Shóyínká.

Name	Type
1. Akogun	= Oyè
2. Olúwolé	= Àbíso
3. Akínwandé	= Àbíso
4. Babtúndé	= Àbíso
5. Olúndèhìn	= Àbíso
6. Ìsòlá	= Oríkì
7. Sóyínká	= Àbíso (family name)

From the above demonstration, it can be seen that there are two normal types of Yorùbá names that are Àbíso and Oríkì. Number one belongs to the category of Oyè which he received in recognition of his achievements and activities. Number two through five are Àbíso names while number six is Oríkì. The number seven, the family name, also belongs to the category of Àbíso. There is no Àmútòrunwá and the absence of foreign names has been rejected, suppressed or he was deliberately not given any one. The Àníjé is also conspicuously absent but is known fact that the laureate has many of this.

Name	Pronunciation	Meaning

From Heaven

Names from heaven by the child are solely detected at birth.

Exercise #1. Now match each name description with the correct Àbísọ́ name.

Abisọ Name	Pronounciation	Meanings to be Matched
Òjó	oh-joe	Born after Etaoka
Àiná	eye-nah	Male child born with umbilical cord around his neck
Àjayí	ah-jah-yee	Born after Otunla
Dàda	dah-dah	Born after ola
Ìgè	ee-gay	Born of mother who sees her period throughout the pregnancy
Táíwò	tie-woe	Born after Idowu
Kèhíndé	kay-hid-day	Born with plenty of hair
Ìdòwú	ee-dough-woo	Born face down, as if praying
Òla	oh-la	Female child born with umbilical cord around her neck
Òtunla	oh-tune-la	Born after twins
Ètaòkọ	eh-taoo-co	First born of twins
Èriòkọ	air-ee-oh-coo	Born feet-first (breech-birthed)
Ìlòrí	ee-lore-ee	Second born of twins

215

Exercise # 2

List five of the following names. Then state the circumstances that surround them (i.e.) The meaning of the name, etc.

1.   Orúkọ Oyè/Orúko Àdàpè

2.   Orúkọ Àbisọ

3.   Orúko Àbíkú

4.   Orúkọ Oríkì

5.   Orúkọ àmútòrun wá

6.   Orúkọ Àjejì

7.   Orúkọ Àníjé or Orúkọ ìnagijẹ

8.   Orúkọ Ifá

The author`s page

Types of Colors

(White) àwò funfun   ◆

(Blue) àwọ̀ buluu   ◆

(Yellow) àwọ̀ yelo/awo esur   ◆

(Purple) àwọ̀ popu   ◆

(Red) àwọ̀ pupa bi ata   ◆

(Black and Shine) awọ dúdú máa dán   ◆

(Gold color) awọ wùrà   ◆

(Pink) àwọ̀ painki   ◆

(Orange) àwọ̀ osàn   ◆

(Brown) àwọ̀ yanrìn   ◆

(Gray) àwọ̀ eérú   ◆

(Green) àwò ewé   ◆

COLOR EXERCISE

1.   What is the correct English word for the following colors. Draw a heart

picture, then paint each with correct color.

1.   Yélò/awo èsúrú

2.   Pópù

3.   Wúrà

4.   Búlùù

95 Wooden housepost representing a woman in an unusually curvilinear stance, bought by the author in Oyo whither it was claimed to have been brought by refugees from Old Òyó which collapsed in 1837. Ife Museum. Ht of figure: 40½ in. Ht of post: 78 in.

5. Funfun

6. Pupa bi'ata

7. Painki

8. Dúdú máa dán

9. Yanrìn

10. Osàn

11. Wúrà

12. Eérú

13. Àwọ ewé

Exercise 2

1. What's your favorite color?

2. What is àwò yanrìn?

3. What is àwọ búlû?

4. What is àwọ osàn?

5. What is àwọ pupa? (Bí ata)

Examples of Sentence Construction with the Use of Colors

Exercise 3

1. Fún mi ní – Give me

   Fún mi ní bàtà dúdú – Give me the black shoe

2. Mo ní – I have

   Mo ní bàtà pupa – I have a red shoe

220

YORUBA DRUM 5, Nigeria

221

3.   Mo rí – I saw

Mo rí ẹiye funfun – I saw a white bird

Now construct your <u>ten</u> sentences by using the above examples.

Exercise 4

Write the English translation of the following sentences.

1.   Fún mi ní ata pupa bí èjè

2.   Fún mi ní fìlà aláwọ pópù

3.   Fún mi ní ewé aláwọ ọsàn

4.   Fún mi ní kẹkẹ aláwò yélò

5.   Fun mi ní owó aláwọ ewé

6.   Mo ní bàtà aláwọ búlúù

7.   Moní bàtà aláwọ yanrìn

8.   Mo ní gèlè pupa

9.   Mo ní garawa funfun

10.   Mo ní ojú dúdú

11.   Mo ra àga dúdú

12.   Mo ra ìwe aláwọ eérú

13.   Mo ra ọgèdè aláwọ yélò

King Shohun of Ogbomosho
1981.

FÍFÍ ỌBA JẸ: THE MAKING OF A KING

After three to six months that a king had died (wàjà or kú) then the (afọbaje) the crowning committee will be meeting to discuss about when to have another king. The Afobajes will then contact the royal family they will like to let them know the next person who has the right to be crowned. The desire to become king always motivates a lot of people from the royal family to compete or to run for the throne. If many people from the royal family to compete or to run for the throne. If many people from the royal family registered to run, the (Afọbajẹ) know the way to investigate each potential candidate. They will go and consult an Ifa priest, or renowned traditional therapist to choose one or elect the best one out of many candidates for the throne. Before a king is crowned, it is the tradition in many cities in Yoruba land that the palace aafin must not be left empty, and there must be an acting king in the palace as well. This is why an old lady is elected to keep the palace works going. Likewise, they may elect a young lady in the Yorùbá land.

After a potential king is elected, his name will be taken to the (Afobajes) Crowning committee to approve the choice. The Afọbajẹ may approve or disapprove of the candidate elected due to the advice they might have received from many dignitaries in the town. However, if the Afọbajẹ say yes that is the end of it. Then the Afọbajẹ will send the name of the king or (ọba) elect to the local government for authorization. After the local government authorization, the day for

88 Bronze head of the late period of Benin art; a massive casting intended to support an ivory tusk on an ancestor altar in the Palace. The projecting decorations on the crown are said in Benin to have been introduced by the Oba Osemwede (1816–48). The head cannot therefore be earlier than this time. British Museum. Ht. 20⅛.

89 The late King of Benin, Oba Akenzua II, photographed during the *Emobo* ceremony in 1959. He wears a crown and collar of coral beads similar to those represented in the bronze head in *Ill. 88*. His shirt is also of coral beads. He strikes an ivory bell and wears ivory armlets and has low-relief plaques of ivory round his waist.

crowning the new king will be set. However, this process may still be kept a secret from the king elect.

On the coronation day, all the royal family members are present. The whole town comes to the palace, and the chairman of the crowning committee makes a short speech. After this speech, a member of Emila, the medicine cult will take off the cap of the Ọba and cover his head with Akòko leaves. Then, and only then, is the elect made aware that he is a king. After the leaves are applied, the king is given a royal hand fan (abẹ̀bẹ̀).

After initiation of the coronation in the palace, the new king elect will be taken to a chief's house called Òdọ̀fin or Ọ̀tún Ìwẹ̀fà as it is known in Òyó. The king elect will be there for three months since he cannot stay in the regular palace immediately after he was elected.

Again the people will gather from near and far on the day the new king moved from the Odofin's residence. This celebration involves drumming, singing, and rejoicing. The new king moves into the palace for the first time after his election. He enjoys cold baths from beautiful women, the finest wardrobe and plenty of food.

Before the king enters the palace, elders prepare three large covered bowls made out gourds (igba). One bowl contains salt, the other ashes and the third contains a mixture of sand, soil and palm oil. After settling down for a while, the king will have to choose amongst the three bowls. If he chooses the bowl that contains salt, this signifies a positive prediction that the new king's reign will be pleasant and peaceful. If the new king chooses the bowl that contains the ashes, this

Farming with hoes

227

signifies that his reign will be full of death and destruction. If the king chooses the bowl of mixture, he will be internalized by his people and supported during his reign.

After the king makes his choice, the elders accompany him to his throne. Once on the throne, the Yorùbá rejoice and sing, they sing and greet the new king as:

KÁBÍYÈSÍ ! |

Ọba Aláṣẹ èkejì òrìsà !

Kí adé pẹ́ lórí !

Kí bàtà pẹ́ lẹ́sẹ̀ |

Kí igba ìrẹ dára fún gbogbowa !

This simply means: Your majesty, your highness, may the crown stay long on your head. May the royal shoe stay long on your feet. May your time on the throne bring peace and transquility to us.

Then the king is led to important places in the palace. One of the important places is the grave of his forefathers who reigned and died. He must visit this place to pay his respect and honor to these dead kings. After this, the king elect will come over to the throne where he will be officially crowned. Dressed in royal garment, he will then handled the beaded shoes, necklaces, beaded staff and staff (walking stick).

After being crowned, the king will give acknowledgments to all the people who prepared the coronation. This will be his first address to the whole town. During this address, he will let the town's people know his agenda during his reign. Then the king will be given the big party for himself and the townsfolks. This is an all week celebration, which involves dancing, feasting, and gift giving.

Ọba Aláàfin Ọ̀yọ́

Ọládìgbólù Kínní, The Ọba Aláàfin of Ọ̀yọ́

210. *Staff with handle and cowrie shells, Eshu cult. 19"*

211. *Ivory head of Eshu (odousa). 2½"*

212. *Ivory clapper (iroke). 14"*

213. *Head of Eshu with cowrie shells (odousa). 3½"*

214. *Bowl for Ifa divination (adjelefa). 6"*

215. *Bowl for Ifa divination (adjelefa). 6½"*

216. *Divination board (okoua-Ifa). 15"*

The wives of the king praise and congratulate him on his election. After the party, the king will go back to his palace to perform sacrifices. Now the king can give orders to both young and old, and he will be held in the highest esteem.

Exercise

1. Describe the status of a candidate for kingship.

2. What are the functions of the king makers (Afobajes)?

3. What are the moral characteristics of a royal candidate?

4. What does Kabiyesi mean?

5. Briefly describe the important places a newly crowned king must visit in the palace.

6. Why should a royal candidate select a bowl? What is the importance of this practice?

7. Do you wish you are a king? Why or why not?

Kábíyèsí

Ọba Aláiyé14wà

231

1.   Adverbs are words that modify verbs in clauses or adjectives and numerals

in nominal group. Some examples are:

Láilái - Forever

Dára dára or dáadá   very well

Pátá pátá - completely

Dúdú - black

Púpọ̀ - very much

Pérẹ́ - only

Funfun - white

Gẹ́gẹ́ - alike

Gidigidi - very

Kùnnùnùn - sluggishly

Kán kán - quickly

Fíó fíó - very high

San san - uprightly

2.   The use of the above adverbs in sentences.   The adverbs are hereby

underlined.

Olọ́run wa <u>lailai</u> - God exist forever.

Ó fo aṣọ nâ <u>dáadáa</u> - she washed the cloth very well.

Àwọn ọmọ jẹ oúnjẹ nâ tań pátápátá - The children finished the food completely.

Dúdú máa dań ni olùfémi - My love is black and shine.

Mo féràn omo mi púpò - I love my child very much.

Ọdún méji péré ni mo fi parí ẹ̀kọ́ mi - It took me only two years to finish my education.

Aṣọ nâ funfun nini - The cloth is snow white.

Ilé nâ dúró sansan - The house stands uprightly.

Gégé bí mo tińsọ - As I was saying.

Inú mì dùn gidigidi - I am very happy.

Adé ńrìn kùnnùnùn - Ade walks sluggishly.

Túndé ńṣeré nínú Òkùnkùn biribiri - Tunde is playing in the dark.

3. Also, there are some other groups of words that can modify verbs.   These are:

Nominal Groups

1. Adverbial which are Nominal Groups

    1. Bìkíta - care

    2. Títí - towards

    3. Ní lóọ́lọ́ yi - very recently

    4. Ní ìgbà láilái - once upon a time

    5. Bóyá - perhaps

    6. Tọwọ́ tẹsè - hand and feet

233

7. Nígbàgbogbo or ní ìgbà gbogbo – always

8. Nítorí - because

9. Tóótọ́ - truly

10. Tayọ̀tayọ̀ - with joy

Examples:

Òjò rọ̀ ní lóólọ́ yi - It rained recently.

Bàbá á dé títí alẹ́ - Father will be back towards evening.

Nígbogbo ìgbà ni inú Olórun ńdùn - God is happy always.

Nítorí Rẹ ni mo se ńsako - I am bragging because of you (referring to God).

Ilé jìnnà ní tòótọ́ - Home is truly far away.

Nwọ́n gba ọ̀rọ̀ nâ tayọ̀tayọ̀ - They took the matter with joy.

Nwọ́n dée towótesè - They tied his hands and legs.

4. Adverbs of time

Adverbs of time expressing the idea of recurrence or repetition are formed by reduplicating the first syllable of a noun expressing time, and then prefixing "li" or "ni".

Examples:

(Ọjọ/day:) "Lí/Ní"/ ojoojọ́, (or) Lọjoojọ́ - Day after day, (Lójoojúmọ́) = every day

(Ọsẹ̀ - week) or losoose - weekly

(Osù - month) or lósoosù - monthly

(Ọdún - year) or lọ́dọọdún - yearly

Africa's Nobel Laureates

Africa had a total of ten Nobel laureates since 1901 when this prestigeous prize was first awarded in the name of Sweden's dynamite magnate, Alfred Nobel.

In 2001 UN Secretary General **Kofi Annan** became the sixth African to receive the Nobel Peace Prize for his own and the UN's endeavors. **Nelson Mandela** and **FW de Klerk** were joint recipients in 1993 for their role in terminating apartheid and laying the foundation for a new nonracial South Africa.

In 1984 Bishop **Desmond Tutu** was honored in his capacity as General Secretary of the South African Council of Churches for his unifying role in the struggle against apartheid. He was preceded by Egyptian President **Anwar Sadat** who was recognized, together with Israeli Prime Minister Menachem Begin, for his contribution to peace in the Middle East.

The first African recipient of the Nobel Peace Prize was **Albert John Luthuli**, who led the non-violent campaign for civil rights in South Africa.

In 2004 Kenya's **Wangari Maathai** was honored with the peace prize for her contribution to sustainable development, democracy and peace.

First of four African winners of the Nobel prize for literature is the Nigerian playwright, **Wole Soyinka**, who was honoured in 1986. He wrote what was characterized by critics as some of the finest poetical plays ever written in English.

In 1988 Egyptian novelist **Naguib Mahfouz** was awarded the literary prize for his short stories and novels depicting urban life.

In 1991 South Africa's **Nadine Gordimer** received the literary prize for her novels and short stories in which the consequences of apartheid formed the central theme.

In 2003, another South African, **John Maxwell (JM) Coetzee** was awarded the literary prize. The fundamental theme of his novels is also apartheid, which in his view could arise anywhere.

Desmond Tutu

Albert Luthuli

Nelson Mandela

Anwar Sadat

FW de Klerk

Kofi Annan

Nadine Gordimer

Wole Soyinka

Wangari Maathai

Naquib Mahfouz

JM Coetzee

Youraba Dress Dasiki

Youraba dress Agbada

(Ìgbá - time) or nígbà gbogbo - everytime or nígbogbo ìgbà

5. The Comparative Degree of Adverbs

This is expressed by placing "ju" "julo" after the positive.

Example:

ga/tall	gajù/taller	gajùlo/tallest
kéré/small	kéréjù/smaller	kéréjùlọ/smallest
fè/wide	fèjù/wider	fèjùlo/widest
mó/clean	mójù/cleaner	mójùlọ/cleanest

Exercise:

1. List four examples of "jù" "jùlọ" adverbs.

2. Employ five of these adverbs in a sentence.

3. List five adverbial nominal groups

4. List five adverbs of time.

5. Demonstrate the comparative degree of adverbs.

71 Pottery sculpture for the altar of Ifijioku, the giver and protector of yams, from the Riverain Igbo village of Osisa west of the River Niger. This is one of several examples taken to England about 1880. The man's wives hold their children while other figures beat a gong, carry a box of offerings and sacrifice an animal. The lids of the offering box and of the rectangular chest in front of the group are both removable. Nigerian Museum, Lagos. Ht 19 in.

Here are some ideas of the animals known to exist in this part of Africa. However, some of them may not have been seen in the zoological gardens of many countries, or in any other collection. The most remarkable of these creatures is the well known Chimpanzees, that are found in several of the larger forests of south western Nigeria. The full grown male chimpanzee is nearly four feet in height. They defend themselves with their tasks, which are truly formidable; and their strength is so great that the Yoruba people consider him as more than match for men. They are generally seen on the trees, making prodigious leaps from branch to branch, and exhibiting all the habits of other monkeys. The face of the young chimpanzees are remarkably human-like, but after the appearance of the husks, it becomes disgustingly prognathous.

Hyenas are rather common, the ajako or wild dog are noiseless creatures, they usually prowl in solitude. Lions can be found in Barba and northern and north eastern part of Òyó, such as oke ogun and Ibarapa division. Leopards are common everywhere. Though not so fierce here as in the forests of Liberia and Sierra Leone. They threaten and sometimes seize man even on the farms. There are several smaller animals of the cat-tribe, some of which are spotted like leopards.

Elephants are common on the prairies of Yoruba, and still more numerous in the forest s of Barba. They seldom intrude into farms, and are not regarded as mischievous animals, but the people have considered aversion to meeting them on the plains. The hippopotamus is confined to the deep waters of the Osa and the Niger. I believe the rhinoceros is never seen in this region; but the people have heard of it as existing somewhere in the interior. There are two species of wild boar, the larger of which is said to be very fierce; the smaller kind is frequently killed by men who make hunting their occupation, and brought into market. A species of Hyrar, different from that of the Cape, but uttering a similar shrill cry, is common among the mountain.

This country nourishes several species of Antelope, some of which are very small, while others are twice the size of the common American deer. A species of Buffalo, called in Sierra Leone the "jackass cow" is frequently seen in Yorùbá land, sometimes singly, but commonly in small doves of ten or twelve.

There are many varieties of birds in Yoruba land. Among them are large and small eagles, even though they are rare. There are several kinds of hawks and falcons, some of which are migratory, booted owls, species of vultures, orioles, red and parti-colored sparrow, black mockingbird with orange breasts and beautiful songbirds, swallows; several species of the whippoorwill family, "goat-sucker" of Sierra Leone, larks, various creepers; crows; songbirds; kingfishers, small species of Guinea hen, large and small partridges, quails several species of doves; storks and ajuntants.

Species of tortoise, a small kind may be eight of ten inches in length, which live in Savannah. There are two species crocodiles. The several specimen which I have seen appear to be intermediate between the true crocodile and the alligator. I

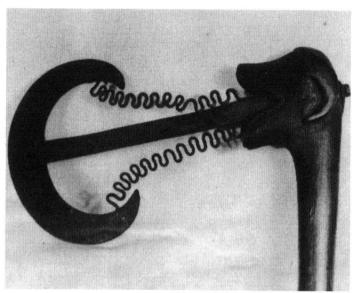

217. *Equestrian figure, Shango cult. 3″*

218. *Head of a ceremonial axe, Shango cult. 16″*

219. *Shango staff (ose-Shango). 23″*

220. *Brass casts with spikes (edan), Ogboni society. 16″*

221. *Water-spirit mask (imole), Ijebu Yoruba. 20″*

222. *Headgear, Egongun society. 18″*

Broad Street
Lagos, Nigeria

saw some of them in the Ògùn river; was probably twelve feet or more in length. Lizards are very numerous; some of them can be compared to the iguana, are two feet long. I have caught and toyed with several chameleons. They creep along very slowly.

Among snakes is the python, the largest of the snakes in Africa. I believe, they never attain a greater length than fifteen feet. Water snakes are not common. However, green snakes and black vipers are the only ones said to be poisonous. I have seen and eaten two kinds of snails, one of which are the Acchatina. They can be seven inches in length. Good oysters are found on the seacoast of the mangrove and kasia trees, presenting a curious spectacle. The principal freshwater shellfish are mussels, resembling the oyster found in the United States and another, found in the rapids for the Ògùn River, precisely similar in appearance to the oyster. The taste is very unsavory.

Insects, and especially flies, fleas, and mosquitoes, are not so numerous as might perhaps be expected. However, ants of several species are in abundance. Ọtà, the species that the Yorùbá people had labeled "the stinger" is frequently useful as an enemy of the termes, which devour every dry vegetable substance within its reach. Another species that is very similar to "ọtà" is called "ijàlọ" or "ijàmànà." They move in countless multitudes, and attack every living thing in their way with the utmost fury.

There are two species of scorpion. The grown black or brown, that is much smaller, but it is said to be more dangerous. I have never been stung by any king of

23 Houseposts carved by a Yorùbá
sculptor in Ketu, Bénin (Dahomey)
and sent as a present from the Alaketu
to the Oni of Ife in 1938. The interlace
designs and the choice of colours are
characteristic of Yoruba sculpture in
Bénin (Dahomey). Ife Museum. Ht
Left: 58 in. Right: 60 in.

245

them, however, my father was stung three times by yellow scorpions, and I know other relatives and friends who have endured painful scorpion sting.

Centipedes are seen in the Yoruba land. I have never heard or known a person that was stung by them. Similarly the elderly still affirm that the spiders of the entire country are harmless like the dreaded and hideous black widow, that are found in the tundra regions in the United States of America.

As I traveled around, I saw innumerable swarms of butterflies. On one December day of 1999, when traveling through the Ògùn River, I met millions of dragonflies, about one fourth of an inch in length, making their way up the town by following the course of the stream. In order to observe all the phases of animal life that this region exhibits, a person must be born or reside there for several years, and visit the forests, mountains and plains at different seasons.

83. *Mask, Guro, Rep. of the Ivory Coast. 9"*

WHAT IS A PREPOSITION?

A preposition is any of a special group of words and phrases such as "in," "on," "over," "instead of," "owing to," which have nouns, pronouns and noun phrases or noun clauses as objects. Yoruba prepositions are composed of nouns and one of these participles, ńí, śí, tí, lí, particles.

Example: #1 'n' particle can be used to mean (in, on, by and under).

Ní iwájú	In the front
Ní orí igi	On the tree
Ní ẹbá ọ̀nà	By the roadside
Ní Orígun	By the corner

Example #2 "si"

'Sí' particle can function as preposition (to, or and)

mo lọ sí oko - I went to the farm.

mo lọ sí ilé - iwe - I went to school.

mo sì ní kó lọ, and - I told him/her to go.

Mo sì ní kó jẹun, and - I told him to eat.

Example #3 "ti"

"Ti", (with, put and it.)

Dúró tì mí - stay with me.

Jókó tì mí - sit with me.

24 Like the houseposts, carved doors may be used in shrines or simply to decorate the house of an important man. This one was collected in Modákeke, Ife. Ife Museum. 50½ × 23 in.

Má dòjú tì mí - Don't put me to shame.

Example #4

Li'- The preceding vowel is usually eliminated when applying particle to answer "when" something happens "where" something had happened. Níbo ni ọmọ wa? - Where is the baby? (Or) ńbo l'ọmọ wà? (Ans) Ọmọ́ wà l'ọ́dọ̀ baba, the baby is with the father. Nígba wo l'odé? - When did you arrive, I arrived yesterday. L'áná ni modé.

VERBS EMPLOYED FOR PREPOSITIONS

Mostly the prepositions can serve as pre-verbs and pre-nouns. These are the verbs employed for prepositions. "ti", "bá", "fi", "fún", "mo", "to", "ka", "lu"

- "ti"

  (1.)   Mo ti mọ̀ - I have known

  (2.)   Mo ti gbọ́ - I have heard

  (3.)   Mo ti jẹun - I have eaten

- "ba" = with, for, from, as in

  (1.)   Ó bá mi lọ - he went with me

  (2.)   Fún = as for, ki mọmọ rẹ fún mi, greet your mọmọ for me

  (3.)   "bá" mi wa aso - help me to look for some cloth

- "fi" (with) to do something with; as in:

  (1.)   ó fi ọbẹ gé ẹran - he cut the meat with a knife

  (2.)   ó fi owó rè pamọ - he kept his money

  (3.)   Ó fi owó pa - he injured his hand

250

258 Repoussé aluminium pa   nting scenes from Yoruba life by Ashiru
Olatunde of Oshogbo. Institu.   Studies, University of Ibadan. Ht 57½ in.

- fúnn to, or, for as in:

  (1.) mo wí fúnn - I told him

  (2.) mò ńsịsẹ́ fúnn - I am working for him

  (3.) Mo rǎ fúnn - I bought it for him

  'Fún' unlike 'ba' and 'fi' is construed as a preposition because 'fún' is always used in the infinitive mode.

- 'mọ́' - to adhere, as in kǎán mọ́gi - nail it to wood; or tee mọ́ lẹ̀ - stepped on his foot.

- 'tọ̀' - (to follow as in) tọ̀ mí wá - come unto me; tọ̀ wọ́n lọ - follow them.

- 'Ka' - to place or set as ń gbé ka lẹ̀ set it on the floor or gbé kaná - put it on the fire.

- 'Lù' - to fall on - as in igi wó lù mí the tree fell on me; or Ọ́ subú lù mí - he fell on me.

Exercise:

- How can particles "n" "si" "ti" and 'le' function as prepositions? List three examples for each particle.

- What are the eight verbs employed for prepositions?

- Construct two complete sentences with each.

COMPOUND PREPOSITIONS

The abstract nouns are frequently employed as adverbs. However, to make them available as prepositions, they must be compounded with ni, =in, si=it, or ti=from, pẹ̀lú, with, or lọ́dọ̀, sometimes ni', is replaced by 'l' and the noun. In other words, compound prepositions are made up of the simple preposition and the object it governs. Examples, ní òde = outside, lóde

Words		Compounded/elison
ní'inú	within, or inside	nínú
ní'ilé	At home	ní'lé
ni òkè	At the top	l'ókè
ní'ìsàlè̩	At the bottom	nísàlè̩
ní'iwájú	At the front	níwájú
ni è̩hìn	behind	léhìn
ní'ò̩tún	At the right	ló̩tún
ní'òsì	At the left	l'osi
wá sí'ilé	Come home	wá'lé
bọ̩' sí'kó̩nàn	Go to the corner	bọ̩' kó̩nàn
jé̩ká gbó̩ ò̩rò̩	please listen	jé̩' á gbó̩ràn
ó' wà ní'sô̩sì	he/she is at the church	o wa n sosi
bàbá wà ní'ilé	bàbá is at home	bàbá wà n̄'lé
bàbá m̄be̩ ní àìn	Bàbá is in the palace	Bàbá m̄be lâàfin
ò̩fé̩ ni ìgbàlà	salvation is free	Ò̩fé̩ nìgbàlà
Bóoti wí lórí'	Just as you said	Bóoti wí lórí'
Bi' ati fé̩ ni ó' rí'	Just as we want it	Báati fé̩ lórí'
Òdì e̩wù ni o wò̩	You wear your clothes inside out	Òdì e̩wù lowò̩
Ní' ibo ni o tı wá'	Where have you been?	Nìbo loti wá'
Ní'bo ni o fi sí'	Where did you keep it?	Ní'bo lo fi sí'

1.   WHAT IS AN ADJECTIVE?

In Yoruba language, adjectives are formed from verbal roots just by adding

the prefix of the verbal root and the vowel "i" which is occasionally replaced by "u"

or "i".

Examples: Verb: Pa: to kill   adjective: pípa: to be killed

Verb: Pọ̀: plenty   adjective: púpọ̀: plentiful

Verb: Jẹ: to eat   adjective: Jíje: to be eaten or edible

Verb: Dùn: sweet   adjective: dídùn: sweeten

Verb: Rà: to rot   adjective: rírà: rotten

2.   The predicate adjectives, are the abstract nouns that are attached to another
       noun by reduplication to indicate quality is performed as in:

   •   Dídùn dídùin lǎa bó yin - Honey is always sweet

   •   Ohun rere - Good thing

   •   Ohun ayọ̀ - Joyful thing

   •   Igi ńlá ńlá - Large trees

   •   Iṣẹ́ wàhálà - A tedious job

   •   Ènìyà alágbára - A strong man

3.   Adjective with clause qualifiers: A clause qualifier is introduced by the
       relative participle, "ti" who, which and a verb as:

Ọbe ti ó mù - A sharp knife

Ọbẹ̀ ti ó dùn - A tasty soup

Igi ti'a dá - A broken stick

Ọmọ ti'o gbé - The child <u>which</u> you stole

4. <u>Adjectives with simple neuter verb as</u>:

Mo ri'ọbọ nla - I saw a large baboon.

Ẹni ọ̀wọ̀ ni o se - You are a Reverend.

Èniyàn're ni ̀dóṣe - You are a good person.

Mo ra ilé ńlá - I brought a larger house.

5. <u>Adjectives by comparison</u>:

This describes the degrees of quality. Answering somewhat to our comparative, are indicated by the addition of words that perform the function of adverbs. The word '<u>jù</u>' is commonly employed for this purpose, i.e., exceedingly good, very good = dáa jù/dára jù.

Example:

1. dára - good   2. dára ju - better   3. dára julo - best

1. ga - tall   2. gajù - taller   3. ga jùlo - tallest

6. **Numeral Qualifiers**

Numeral qualifiers - adjectives are arranged in sets, and they are easily recognized from the sets to which they belong.

Set 1	Set 2	Set 3	Set 4
Méta/three	Mé tèè ta	Méta-méta	Èketa - kẹta
	Both three	three each	Every third

Méjọ / eight	Méjèèjọ	Méjọ méjọ	Èkejọ Kéjọ
	All eight	Eight each	Every eight
Méje / seven	Méjèeje	Méje méje	Èke je kéje
	all seven	Seven each	Every seventh
Méfà / six	Méfèefà	Méfà-méfà	Èkefà kefà
	All six	Six each	Every sixth

7. **Demonstrative Qualifiers**

Eyi-this	Wọnyi- these	Wọnyen- those	Wònni- those
Example: owó	Owó wònyi	Owó wònyen	Owó wònni
Èyi-This money	These money	Those money	Those money

Exercises: Underline the predicate adjectives from sentences (a-d) below.

7.   Which of the following is a predicate adjective?

a)   I saw a large baboon. Mo ri ọbọ ńlá

b)   Badmas is a strong man. Badmus jé alágbára Okùnrin.

c)   I adore children. Mo féràn àwọn omodé

d)   A Reverend. Eni owo

Exercise 2.   Underline the adjectives with relative participle from sentences (a—d) below.

a)   A tasty soup - Ọbè to dùn

b)   The child which you stole - Ọmọ t'ó gbé

c)   A good person - Enirere niô se

d)   A broken stick - Òpá ti o dá

256

Exercise 3.   Define the following and give two examples of each (a-d).

1.   Predicate adjectives

2.   Qualificative adjectives

3.   Adjectives comparison

4.   Adjectives with relative pronouns

Underline Adjectives with simple neuter verbs:

1.   I bought a large house - Mo ra ilé ńlá kan

2.   A large house - Ilé ńlá kan

3.   We want good thing/ Nkàn rere la fẹ́

Yorùbá Coiffures

a: Kòlésè Hairstyle.
b: Ìpàkó Ẹlédè Hairstyle.
c: A Variation of the Panumọ́ Hairstyle.
Author's drawings.

WHAT IS A CONJUNCTION?

A conjunction is a word used to connect words phrases, clauses, or sentences. We cannot do, but refer to verbal roots when we are about to form conjunctions in Yoruba. For example:

1.   (a) And = "àti" is represented by various particles. To connect personal pronouns: The conjunction "àti" must be in the middle of the personal pronoun. "Ìwo àt èmi" / You and me Yíò pa eku àti eiye/will kill the rat and the bird. Àwon àti àwa ló kó dé / Both they and us came first (b) "Asì" is another particle of conjunction.

Example: "a rí asì muu" / we saw him, and we caught him:, a je asì mu" / we ate and drank, " a lo asi bò"/ we went and came, "a pe okuhrin, asì pe obìnrin' / we invited both men and women> Note that both àti, asì, ósi are employed to connect nouns, pronouns, adverbs, and prepositions. (c) Ódìde ósì to baba rè lo / He rose and went to his father (d) "on" and "pelu" and "si" are another word for "àti" and in all respects are being used as follows:

"On or oun" - Mo rí Tundé òn Gàni'- (I saw Tunde and Gani) Múrí òn egbon re ti jeun/Múrí and his brother have eaten.

1.   'Pèlú' - is frequently employed in the place of and, to connect nouns and occasionally pronouns. As omo pèlú iya re lódé / (the child and his mother have come). Èmi pèlú won ni yíó lo / (me and them will go).

Ifá is the oracle of divination who mediates between the gods and men. The gods are believed to communicate their motives through the process of divination. The priest is able to suggest actions that will avert misfortune. Through Ifa divination an individual, or whole town, can obtain solutions to difficult problems and restore good relations between themselves and the gods.

Eshu-Elegba is the messenger of the gods. He is the youngest, most agile, and quick witted. He causes trouble for those who neglect the other gods. It is Eshu who delivers the sacrifices that have been prescribed by the Ifa diviner to Olorun, the distant high god. Eshu and Ifa are therefore intimates in the business of manipulating the destinies of men. Eshu is the only deity acutally portrayed in Yoruba art. It is Eshu's face that is represented on many Ifa divination boards and occasionally on objects used by all the other cults. In character with his contradictory nature, Èshu dance staffs (ogo Elegba) are frequently held head downward.

Eshu's long, phallic hairstyle is regarded as the "sign" of his bond of friendship with Ifa, the god of divination. In one story, Ifa pretended he was dead in order to test the devotion of those around him. He was disappointed by everyone except Eshu. Even though the trickster god was in the process of shaving his head, he was so overcome by grief with the news that he rushed to Ifa's bedside with his hair half shaved. Ifa recognized his friend's faithfulness and asked Eshu to continue to let his hair grow in this half-shaved style forever.

Eshu figures are usually decorated with beads and cowries, but the god may also be symbolized by a simple chunk of uncarved stone. The Meyer Collection figurative stone sculpture depicted here may be an exceptionally rare shrine piece. It depicts Eshu seated on a stool. Carved in a terse, compact style, only half of its length is discolored, suggesting that it had once been buried in the ground.

http://www.yorubareligion.org/gallery/anc.html

259

2. "Sì" is another conjunction that is employed to connect verbs only as dìde, sì lo / arise and go. Dìde sì korin / arise and sing. Ìwo àti èmi ri - a sì kìi / you and I saw him/her and greeted him.

3. "Because is represented by nítorítí àánú rè dúró laílaí, / "(for his mercy endureth forever)". Because denotes by reason of either of the two may be employed at the option of the speaker; (i.e.) let's go home because it is about to rain. / (Jékà lo sí lé, nítori'ti ójò mbò).

4. Before, / "ki'o tó, " or kín tó, (before / (sin mi), as in (he finished before me)" o pari'sin mi.

5. "But" sùgbón, "as in / mo péé sùgbón ko gbò/, I called him but he did not hear me.

6. Bìkòse, (i.e.) "Kí ìse òmùgò bìkòse Ologbón, "He is not a fool but a wise man.

7. "Bá", as bi'ó bá rí'ejò, yio ho. If he sees the snake, he will run.

8. Lest, / "ki ma baa: as ànsisé ki a má bà sagbe" (or) ("Àn sisé ki'á Mà bà jalè)."

9. Neither...nor kò or kìi'sùn, bénì kìi'tòògbé/ He neither sleep nor slumber. Sometimes we can use "òn kò" as in kò je béèni kò mu," (He neither eats not drinks), or kò ni'ìyá béèni/kòní baba (he has neither father nor mother) or,

10. Tàbí (as in) ìwo tàbi'èmi / (you or me), a male or female /, ako mbí abo? Eja mba kan, / positive or negative, (fish is negative, akan is positive) in Yorùbá.

11. Whether....or tàbí or, ìbáà jé, or ìbáà se as in Olórun fe gbogbo ènìyàn,

ìbáààjẹ́ okùnrùn, ibaajẹ̀ obìnrin, ìbáà jẹ ọmọdé tàbí àgbà / That is, God love, all people whether men or women, whether children or adult.

12. Since nígbàtí iná ti dé ni mo ti ńgbádùn/ I have been feeling better since the power is back, or I have not gone anywhere since you left/ N kòtíì lo sibikibi nigbati o ti lọ.

13. "That" is represented by several particles: (i.e.) "Kì", 'ti', "pe" "nje", "bi"/ that

    1. ("kì") ki o (as) mo ni "ki" o maa lo, I said that he must go.

    2. ("Tí"), kin ni emi o se "ti" èmi yíò fi jógún aiyé. What shall I do to inherit life?

    3. ("Pé") as / o rìí pé o dára. He saw that it was good (or) Tọ́ ọ wò kí o sì ri "pé" rere l' Olúwa; Try Him and you will see that God is good.

14. Njẹ́/Then, ǹjẹ́, a kò ní jẹun sùn ni yẹn. Then we will not have dinner?

15. "Though" "bí" this particle is frequently followed by bí ótilẹ̀ jẹ́pé (i.e.) Though we were late, still we have seats / (Bíó'o tilẹ̀ jẹ́pé a pé, a túń rí ìjókó)

Exercise:

a) List the sixteen verbal roots we have to refer to when we are about to form conjunctions.

b) Construct two sentences with each of these verbal roots as they were used in the chapter.

What Is Number in Grammar?

Number is the representation in a language, by inflection or otherwise, of singleness or plurality. How do we know that a noun is plural since Yorùbá language does not have the singular and plural numbers?

There are two methods of indicating that a noun is plural:

1.   By using the personal pronoun "awon" or nwon before the noun. Unlike English language where plurals are differentiated through the use of 's' or 'they', them, those, etc.

   a)   Àwọn ọmọ ńkọrin/ the children are singing.

   b)   Jẹ́ kí àwọn ẹran jẹun / let the animals eat.

   c)   Àwọn ọkùnrin dà? / Where are the men?

   d)   Jẹ́kí àwọn obìnrin jokǒ / Let the women sit down.

   e)   Pe àwọn obìnrin wolé / call all the women in.

   f)   Àwọn akọrin dà? / Where are the choir?

   g)   Àwọn àsàyàn orin / the selected hymn.

   h)   Ibùjókǒ àwọn ẹlẹ́gàn / the seat of the scornful.

   i)   Àwọn ará ìgbànnì gbọ́n / the ancients were wise.

   j)   Àwọn àgbàlagbà ní Òye / Elderly people have wisdom.

2.   The ideas of reciprocity and plurality are occasionally expressed by reproduction and a copulative conjunction; as

a)   Ọ̀rẹ́ kí/ya ọ̀rẹ́ - friends are always together / or ore oun ore kija / Friends do not fight with each other.

b)   Ọdoodún - every year

c)   Gbogbo - (all) - gbogbo aiyé, the whole world.

d)   In the numerals, plurality is indicated by reduplicating the first portion; as in

e)   Ogboogbọ̀n - in thirties

f)   Ogoogójì̱ - in forties

g)   Ẹgbẹgbèrún - in thousands

h)   Ogoogún - in twenties

Exercise:

1.   How do we know a noun is plural, give five examples of these plural nouns.

2.   List three examples of reproduction in copulative conjunction.

CASE

WHAT IS CASE?

Case in grammar is the syntactical relationship of a noun, pronoun or adjective. There is no inflexion of the Yorùbá noun to indicate case. However in calling to a person at a distance the particle "O" is often employed after the noun as:

1.   Ẹ̀yin ọmọ mi Ò! - O my children!
2.   Bàbá Búkáyọ̀ O! - Bukayo's father!
3.   Akíntúndé Ó! - Akíntúndé!
4.   Olú-bùnmi O! - Olúbùnmi!

2.   If the person being addresed is not far off, the speaker use article "the" / "n̂a" as obinrin n̂a dé, the lady has come.

•   Ọmọ n̂a dé - The child has come

- Ilé <u>ná</u> wó lulè - the house has fallen down
- Isé <u>nâ</u> ti parì - the job is done
- Ọmọ bihrin nâ lẹ́wà - the girl is beautiful

3. In addition one who is quite near to the speaker, the demonstration "yi" "this" is frequently employed as:

1. Ọmọdé yí wúlò - this child is useful
2. Omi yi kò dára - this water is bad
3. Ilé yì dára - this is a beautiful house
4. Ọkùnrin yi le pariwo - this man is too loud
5. Ọmọ yi kúro lóna - this child get out of the way

4. The possessive relation is expressed in the following ways; the name of the possessor always follows that of the thing possessed, as:

1. Ìwé Adé - Ade's book
2. Ilé ìyá - mother's house
3. Ilé ebí - family hosue
4. Ile eiye - bird's nest (or) Ile eiye
5. Èbádò etí kun - the seashore river side
6. Ọpá irin - an iron staff

Exercise:

1. What particles can we use while calling a person at a distance.

2. Employ these particles in five separate categories.

3. Demonstrate how possessive relations are expressed in five sentences.

Interjections

Interjection is a word expressing emotion or simple exclamation.

The Yoruba principle interjections are as follows:

Ah!; Ye!; Oh!; Aa!;=alas!

Sáwò ó!; Wo!; K´ yesii!;=Behold!

Hun!; Eh!; Kai!;=Fudge!

Síọ̀!; Ooh!;=Shaw!

Dákẹ́!; Sinmin!;=Be Quiet!

Ẹepà!; Móńdàla!;=Wonderful!

Àgò!; Bìlà!; Kúrò!;=Get out of the way!

Exercise:

1.   List seven Yorùbá principle interjections.

2.   Employ each of them in expressing emotion or exclamation.

Have an African Wedding!

ÒWE ÀTI Ọ̀RỌ̀ ÌJÌNLẸ̀ YORÙBÁ

SPECIMEN OF THE YORÙBÁ PROVERBS AND IDIOMATIC

EXPRESSIONS

Yorùbá language abound in proverbs, some of them sound like poetry, while some of them serve as moral science. Yoruba proverbs are intellectual observation on the nature of things, and they are inventive ability of reflection on the law of nature. Some of these proverbs are designed to indicate the various relative duties of men, women and children; while a few are simply ingenious play on words. Attempt to list some examples of these proverbs are not only to exhibit the philosophy of the Yorùbá language, but to illustrate the character of the "African Minds", Yorùbá Example:

1. Àdábá nì'jà, eni 'ijà ò bá nii pe'rarè l'ọ́kùnrin

    Fight is always unpredictable, if you are not involved in fighting yet you will be boasting of your strength.

2. Òbàiyéj'ẹ́ kò sée 'fi' di ọ̀rọ̀ hàn

    It will not do to reveal one's secrets to a tattler.

3. Alátiṣe nií mọ àtise ara rẹ̀

    Client centered therapy. Individual has the ability to resolve problems.

4. Àbàtá ta kété bi'ẹni kò b'odò tan

    The mash stands aloof as if it were not akin to the stream-said of the people

266

who are proud and reserved.

5. Àgbà kìi wà lójà, kórí ọmọ titun wọ́

   In the presence of elderly person(s), conflicts should not go unresolved.

6. Ebi kò pa Ìmòle, Ó ní óun Kìije àáyá, b' ́ebi bá paṢule yio jẹ ọbọ

   When a Muslim is not hungry, he says he will not eat monkey, but when he

   is hungry he will eat a baboon (i.e., he's not so scrupulous)

7. Alábahun tó gbọ́n sásá, Ikú ńpaa, átóńtóri ọpòló tóji tón gbéra rẹ sánlẹ̀ kólójọ́ –

   ó tóó dé·

   The tortoise that is so clever still dies, how much less the frog that bounces

   itself on the ground everyday, won't it almost die before it time comes.

8. Pipé ni yio pẹ, akílòló yio pe baba

   It may be long, however, a starmara will eventually call daddy.

9. Amúni sẹ̀sín ẹ̀tẹ̀ tii mu ni lógòńgóo imú

   Making one to be disgraced; leprosy which attacks one on point of nose.

10. Ìji kìijà, kó gbé odò lọ

    No matter how strong the storm, it cannot take the river along.

11. Àkùkọ gàgàrà ni dájó fun ni laa rin ̀ogànjọ́

    A large cock decides for us in the midst of the night. (The proverb may be

    quoted when a dispute is suddenly decided by unexpected evidence.

12. Àkọbí n t'elẹran

    The first-born is the shepherd's (Traditionally, when a soman takes she'goat

    (an ewe) (both of which are termed eran) she claims the first-born lamb for

her own.

13. Ọ̀rọ̀ tííjẹ́ owó, ẹgbàá ìdọ̀bálẹ̀ kòlé tań an

   *The problem that requires money, two thousand prostrations will never solve
   it.*

14. Asúré nínú ẹ̀ẹkan kíi sojú asán, bi'kò bá lé ǹkan, ǹkan ńlee

   *An adult that runs around in the bush, if he's not running after something,
   something is running after him.*

15. Akíi bínu orí, ká fi fìlà dé i

   We cannot despise the head by using the cap to cover the butt.

16. Akíi wá aláṣọ àlà ni''ṣo elépo pupa

   *We do not look for a man clad in white cloth in the quarters of the palm-oil
   seller.*

17. Òkété ni ọjọ́ gbogbo ni óun mọ̀, òun kò mọ ọjọ́ miràn

   *The rat says he knows everyday, but he does not know another day (i.e., he
   lays up nothing for the future.*

18. Ojúkòkòro baba ọ̀kánjúà

   Covetousness is the father of unsatisfied desires.

19. Ológbò baba àrọ̀kiń

   The cat is the father of traditionists.

20. Alágbára má mèrò baba ọ̀lẹ

   *A strong person who is destitute or forthought is the father (or prince) of
   laziness.*

21. Ẹni ti kò gbọ ti ẹ̀gà, tó ní ẹ̀gà ńpa tótó ẹnu

One who does not understand the oriole, says the oriole is noisy, or merely chattering. (The meaning of the proverb is that men are prone to despise what they do not understand).

22. Eláda èdá l'Ọlọrun dá ni

God has created us with different natures or dispositions; hence we should not expect to find the same qualities in everyone.

23. Bi alágbara bá jẹ ọ ni yà, kió fẹrín síi

If a great man should wrong you, smile at him because resistance would bring you a still greater misfortune.

24. Alápatà kò mọ irú ẹran

The butcher has no regard for the breed of the sheep (which he kills). He attends to his own business and does not meddle with matters which does not concern him, i.e. Animal care.

25. Igbó biribiri, Òkùnkùn biribiri, bópẹ, bóyá òkùnkùn ni yio sète igbó

The forest is dark, and the night is dark, however, the darkness of the night will soon conquer that of the forest.

26. Osàn t' ori gbajúmọ ti kò bọ, bópẹ bóyá eiyẹ oko ni ofi jẹ

The ripe orange that refuses to fall before the great man, eventually the birds of the farm will eat it up. (A beautiful woman that refuses to marry a great man, eventually she will suffer in the hand of a very poor man).

27. Bi kò báwa se ọbùn ènìà, tani ìbá jí lówùrọ ki o ma bọ ojú rẹ mọ sàsá

Except a sloven, who will rise up in the morning without washing his face
nicely.

28. Èmú ni balè̩ àgbè̩de̩

Tongs are the governor of blacksmithing. The tongs are at the head of the
blacksmith's shop; because they control the hot iron which otherwise would
be unmanageable.

29. O̩s̩ó̩ oníbùijé ko pe 'sàn, o̩s̩ó̩ onínàbì kò jo dúnlo̩

The marks made by the buje woman does not last nine days; the marks made
by the inabi-woman does not last more than a year. (No advantage or
possession is permanent).

30. Bí ajá bá l'é̩ni lé̩hìn á pa o̩bo̩

If a dog has his comrade behind him, he will kill a baboon – this proverb is
designed to show that "Unity is Strength."

31. Àìkó̩ ìwó̩rìn ejò, níí s̩e 'kú pa wó̩n

Snakes get killed easily because they don't walk in group. (The proverb is
pleading for unity among people).

32. Àg̩bájo̩ o̩wó̩ ni a fí ńs̩o̩ àyà

The united fingers are effective in boasting. (The proverb is also pleading for
the strength in unity).

33. Ajá tí kò ní etí, kò s̩ée fí dé̩gbè̩

A heedless dog will not do for hunting. (If a person will not take advice, no
one will employ or trust him/her).

34. Ibi pelebe lǎa fi àdá lélè

A cutlas is laid down flat always.

35. Okùn omo ìyá yi

The rope that ties siblings together is durable. (You cannot under estimate the strength of family ties).

36. Oni' lé njε pòpòndó álejò ni'ki a se òun lówó kan èwà

The host is surviving on wild beans, the guest expects a handful of boiled popular beans.

37. Má gbékè lé ogún, towó eni nií tó ni

Trust not in inheritance; the product of one's hand is sufficient for one – Said to those who neglect industry because they expect to inherit property.

38. Àkosèbá, eyi ti je o dun

He who waits for chance, may wait a year – Said to those who are "waiting" for something to turn up.

39. Eni tó ran ni ní' sé ni aaberu, a kìi bèrù eniti a ran ni sí

We should fear him who sends us with message, not to whom we are sent (applied to messengers sent from one king or chief to the subjects).

40. Èrò pèsèpèsè, kò mò pé ara ńkan ìgbin

It may be convenient for the rich, but you do not understand the suffering of the poor.

41. Ohun tia fi èsò mú ki bàjé; ohun ti a fagbára kankan mú níile

An affair that is conducted with gentleness is not married; but an affair that

271

is conducted with violence causes vexation.

42. Ìkónkósó tiri pa eku, ìwò tiiripa ẹja', bómọdé yio bagbà jẹun ńtiri ńiitiri

A trap bends in order to kill a rat, the hook bends in an attempt to catch a

fish, therefore, if a child wants to dine with an elderly person, that child

should bend (if you want favor from an elderly person you should show them

respect).

43. À gbá òfìfo ló ndún woroworo

An empty drum makes the loudest noise.

44. F' òkò ńlá pa alóǹgbá, óní bẹ̀ẹ̀ l'ẹni tó juniloo tii ṣeni

Said in illusion to the fact that the strong oppress the weak.

45. A fejú toto kò kan ọkùnrin

Much gesticulation does not prove manliness – "A barking dog does not

bite."

46. Bí kú bańpa gbajúmò eni, òwe l'óńpa fuń ni

When you age mates are dying, it is a clear warning to you that the end is

near.

47. Aláséjù pérẹ́ ńí tẹ́

A self-willed man soon has disgrace. "Pride goes before destruction."

48. Ẹni ti a kò mọ pé yio le pàgó, tóń kóle aláruru

A person that was not expected to build a hut, he has the tallest building in

the community. (You do not underestimate anybody).

49. Owó níí b'ọju òrẹ́ẹ́ jẹ́

It is money that disrupts friendship relationships.

50. Aláràjẹ kò mọduń; abi isúu ta bí'igi

   The buyer does not consider the season, he thinks perhaps yams grow as big

   as logs.

51. Isu tiá tẹnumọ́ kǐ jóná (persistence pays a lot)

   The yam that we check often while on the stove, will not get burnt.

52. 'Ibí' kǐ jù ibi;́ bí'a ti bí'ẹrú laa bi'ọmọ

   One birth does not excel another. As the slave was born, so was the free-

   born child.

53. Wa'gbà àkàrà wá gba dùǹdú, lọmọ kékeré fiń mojú'ẹni

   Sharing small, small edible things with children will impel them to be fond

   of one.

54. A kǐmọ orúkọ alája'ki'á paá'jẹ

   You will not kill the pet of your good neighbor.

55. Kòsi'abiýá enɨto'mọ́

   There is no hand pit that is naturally odorless. (That is "every one has

   skeletons in the closet.")

56. Wèrè dùn uń wò, kò seé bí'l'ọmọ

   It may be fascinating to watch a lunatic in action, but we cannot wish such

   as a child.

57. Àì f'àgbà féníkan kò jáiyé óguń

   There is no organization without leadership.

273

58. À dán doríkodò, ó ńwò ìse ẹiyẹ gbogbo

The bat hangs suspended with its head down, watching the actions of all

birds. (The proverb is probably designed to teach silent observation.)

59. Ẹyin l'ohùn tó bá bọ́ sílè fífọ́ níi fọ́

Words of mouth are like eggs, when they break you can't fix the shell back

together. (Therefore, watch what you say).

60. A kìi fi iná sóri òrùlé sùn

You cannot leave fire on the roof and go to sleep.

61. Ọba' yànjẹ́ ba arạ rẹ̀ jẹ́

He who injurs another, bring injury upon himself.

62. T'ójò bá ńpa òkan ọrẹ́, ó dá milójú pe gbogbo won l'ejí ńpa

When one of the friends is without shelter it is obvious the rest of the friends

are to be discouraged.

63. Abẹ̀bẹ̀ níi bẹ'kú, abẹ̀bẹ̀ ni bà'rùn, bi orú bámú, abẹ̀bẹ̀ níi bẹ̌

Fan dissipates death, fan pleader wards off difficulty, if the heat is severe, a

fan mitigates it. (A fanciful play upon "word" is the principal design of this

proverbial saying). (It also shows the power of entreaty).

64. A kìi bunni jẹ, ká tún bun ni tà

We cannot invite you to dine, then give you some food for sale.

65. Ìwà l'ewà ọmọ ènìyàn

Morality is the beauty of an individual.

66. A kìi kánjú la ọbẹ̀ tó gbónán

You cannot consume hot soup in a hurry.

67. Àì si'nílé ológbò, ilé di 'lé èkúté

When the cat vacates the house, the mice are free to occupy the house.

68. À paà délé'kò jẹ́ ká mọ'lógbò l'ọ́de

A cat is not recognized as a hunter, because it does not bring its kill home.

69. Ewúré ilé'kò mọ yì ọde, ajogún ẹ̀wù Kò mọ iyì agbádá ńlá

A domestic animal does not appreciate it fierce hunter (its owner) just like cloth hier does not appreciate the antique garment.

70. Ipa abẹ́rẹ́'ni okùn rìn

Paths of needle – it is thread follows. The thread follows the needle – (applied to anything that happens as a natural consequences).

71. Adárìjinni ní'ìṣete ejọ́

He that pardons the aggressor, gains the victory in the dispute. Designed to cultivate a forgiving spirit.

72. Abẹ́rẹ́ bọ́ lọ́wọ́ adẹ́tẹ̀, o'dète òrań ba'lè ódèrò

If a needle falls from the mutilated hand of a leper, it requires thought (how to pick it up) if a difficult matter comes on a country, it requires thought (how to avert it).

73. Òṣì níi'jẹ́ tanì'mò ọ́ rí, owó níi'jẹ́ mo bẹ́tan

No one will like to identify himself/herself to a poor person, but when you are successful, people will like to esteem you.

74. Ẹlẹ́dẹ̀ pa òfò tań, ońwá eni rere tí'yio fi ara rẹ̀ .yí

The pig, having done wallowing in the mire, is seeking some clean person to rub against – said of disgraced persons who attempt to intrude themselves upon good society).

75. Ẹnú dùn uń rò'fọ́, agada ọwọ́ ṣe gẹ́gi

It is easier to cook green vegetable by just talking about it, as it is easier to cut a tree down by demonstrating how to cut it with bear hands, (i.e.) It is easier said than done.

76. Ẹni gbẹ́ òkú àparò gbé aápọn

Whoever picks a dead partridge, picks trouble.

77. bàmí Gbàmí! kòyẹ àgbàlagbà ẹranko ńlé mi bọ̀ ko yẹ ọdẹ igbó; èèwò òrìsà

The cry resquei, resque!du benefit an elderly man, just like" an animal is running after me does not benefit a hunter, god forbid!! (This proverb is calling for courage).

78. Ọ̀rọ̀ ṣe ni wò, kalẹ́ meni to fẹni

You will know your friends, when you are in trouble. (i.e.) "A friend in need, is a friend indeed."

79. Enii akò fẹ ni ilẹ́ rẹẹ́ jìnnà

The house of an enemy is always too far away.

80. Bi abá sòkò lójà, ará ilẹ́ nií bá

If we throw a rock in the market randomly, it may land on your relative.

81. Fi'jà fÓlórun jà fọwọ́ lẹ́ràń

Leave the battle to God; and rest your temple on your hand (as spectator).

That is, trust in God's providence.

82. Tinú tinú, tẹ̀hìn tẹ̀hìn ni labaláblá fíi fíyìn f'Ọlọ́dùmarè

   By its beauty, the butterfly praises God within and without. (i.e., in all its

   parts)

83. Afẹ́ jẹran kó pẹ́ lẹ́nu, sùgbọ́n ọ̀nàǹfun kòjé

   We wish we can chew the delicious meat longer. Unfortunately, we have to

   swallow it. Said to end an interesting program on TV or radio.

84. Ògún kò rọ ike, àgbède kò rọ bàtà, okó ṣeé ro àgbèdẹ pọ'kọ́ tà

   Ògún does not work ivery, the smith does not work leather, if the field were

   not difficult to cultivate, the blacksmith would not make shoes to sell – that

   is, every man to his trade.

85. Ikú ogun níi pa akíkanjú, ikú odò ní pa òlùwẹ̀

   A hero always dies at war just like a swimmer dies while swimming.

86. A rí t'eni mọ́ọ́ wí a fi àpáàdì bàràkàtà bo tiẹ̀ mọlẹ̀

   People tend to talk about other people's issues, but cover their own potsherd.

87. Akìigba àkàkà lọ́wọ́ akítì; a kìigba ilé baba ọmọ lọ́wọ́ ẹni

   We cannot cure a baboon from squatting (because it is natural to him). We

   cannot take the homestead from a man; (because it is his, by natural right).

88. Aṣe ọran ikòkò ṣebí oun lan báawi, abi ara 'fu bi ẹni ṣe ohun

   The perpetrator of secret crime thought it is him that they are talking about.

   His face grows pale as if he had done something wrong.

89. Asọ̀rọ̀kélẹ́ bojúwògbẹ́, igbẹ́ kì íṛọ́, ẹni tí a ba sọ fún ní ṣe ikú pa ni

A whisperer watches the bush; the bush never tell secrets; but to whom one speaks is the traitor. (If a person wishes his secrets to be kept, he should not confide them to others).

90. Àmáa lé eló̩yó̩ró̩ jìnnà ká tóó bá adìe̩ wí

Let ele-joro leave before rebuking the hen.

91. Àmáa lé e̩ló̩yó̩ró̩ jìnnà ká tóó bá adìe̩ wí

Let ele-joro leave before rebuking the hen.

(i.e.) (The principal will not rebuke the teacher in front of the students).

92. Akìi dúpé̩ ló̩wó̩ ara e̩nii

You cannot thank yourself. (In Yoruba culture, when a relative says thank you to another one, the receiver of the thanks may say, "When you say thank you to me is like you are thanking yourself because you and I are of the same family).

93. Igi gan gan ran má guń mi ló̩jú, Ò kèerè làá tíi yan

To prevent a thorny stick from entering into your eyes, you need to plan the escape strategy while you watch the stick from distance.

94. Ìsé̩ ìgbòǹsè̩ ko s̩e fí ran o̩mo̩ e̩ni, ojú àwo l'àwó fií gb'o̩bè̩

Marter that is related to the use of toilet cannot be delegated. The plate receive the soup while facing up. (That is, what you must handle by yourself should not be delegated).

95. Bó̩jú bá ye̩'jú k'óhùn má ye̩ ohùn.

If the eyes missed the eyes, the voices should not miss the voices. (i.e.) Even

278

though we are separating, let's keep the communication going.

96. Ohun tó wà léhìn èfà, ój'òje lọ

   What is behind six is more than seven. That is, seven is not the end of numerals. It is used as a warning to teenagers. (i.e.) (There are other responsibilities behind a sexual expression).

97. Ohun t'ánfẹ́ láagọ̀ọ fun

   You endure insults or pain or abuse because of your desired target.

98. Kójú má ńbi, ẹsẹ̀ lòògùn rẹ̀

   For the eyes to stay out of trouble, feet must be in motion.

99. Ajé ni fújà

   Money is the will power.

100. Ìya'ni wúrà, baba ni dígí

   Mother is the gold to the child, while father is the mirror.

101. Ilé ni àpótíi jòko de ìdí

   At home, the chair always awaits the butt.

102. Sòkòtò t'óń sisẹ́ àrań oko l'óńgbé

   You always leave the farm uniform at the farm.

Exercise:

Critically analyze any ten of Yoruba proverbs. Then explain the moral philosophy that each of them exhibits.

THE YORUBA ORAL TRADITION

Oral tradition is another approach to historical knowledge. It has been used

King Oluwo of Iwo
Oshun State Nigeria
1995

by the Yorùbá people even before their language was lettered. Basically, the term means the transmission of facts, values and fiction through storytelling by word of mouth.

The following are examples of "oral tradition" in Yorùbá:

1. Àló àpamò̩ – Riddles and Jokes

2. Alò̩ àpagbè – Story with chorus

Examples

<u>Àló àpamò̩ – Riddles and Jokes</u>

1. There is something that passes the front yard of a king, but does not care to say hello to the king. (This thing is part of nature), What is it? (i.e.) The storyteller – Alo oo (all) aloo Ki lo n kojá lójú de o̩ba ti ko ki o̩ba o (answer). It is an erosion/Àgbàrá òjò̩.(Erosion just flow, it does not greet anybody)

2. There is a small room that is full of thorns. Who knows what it is? (i.e.) Àló̩ o, (all) Àlò̩ò̩, Yàrá Kótópó kìkì ègún (Answer) Mouth!/e̩nu. (You remember our mouth are full of teeth).

3. There is a God of ancient that goes with you everywhere you go. Who knows what it is? (i.e.)Alo̩ o (all) alo̩. Òrìs̩à baba àló̩ kan láélàé, Òrìs̩à baba àló̩ kan l'àèlàè, ibikíbi ni báńii ló̩ o, tani mo̩ o (Answer) – Your shadow/Òjiijìrè.(Your shadow always go with you).

I. Story with Chorus/Àló̩ Àpagbè
Ìjàpá ati Òkéré̩ je̩ ò̩ré̩
Ò̩ré̩ timó̩-timo̩ ni wó̩n

Wọ́n jọ maan jẹun pọ ni

Asíń kii se ọ̀ré won
Ni ojọ́ kan -ijà sẹlẹ̀ láarin Asíń àti Òkéré

Ijapa la ija èrú
Omú Asíń sílẹ̀ fuń Òkèrè láti nà
Inú bi´Asíń gidigidi
O´ gbá ìjàpá mú
Ó sì gée ni imú jẹ
Ìjàpá wa nkorin pé

Solo: Asíń tòun t'Òkéré (all:) jóó mi jo
Solo: Ìjà ni wóń jo ńjà (all:) jóó mi jo
Solo: Ni Asíń ba´ge ni nímúje (all:) jóó mi jo
Solo: Ìtàn réé egbé mì (all:) joo mi jo

Ìgbà tí´imú ÌJàpá gé mọ Asíń lẹnu ni o to fii sílè
Ìdi´rẹ ni yí tí´imú ìjàpá kò fi ju kékeré títi´di òní olóní o!

Translation of Àló Àpagbé/Story with Chorus

The Tortoise and Squirrel were good friends.
They used to eat and go around together.
Rat was not a friend to either.

One day, there was a conflict between the Rat and the Squirrel. They were exchanging blows.
The Tortoise made effort to separate them.
However, the Tortoise had a dubious intention.
He held the Rat's hands so that the Squirrel (his friend) could have the upper hand in the fight.

The Rat was very angry about this.
The Rat then temporarily left Squirrel,
He decided to turn to the Tortoise.
The Rat then bit the Tortoise's nose and swallowed the bite!

The chorus of this stroy is as follows:

Solo: The Rat and the Squirrel (all) Joomi jo
Got into real fighting
Solo: (All) Joo mi jo

Solo: The Rat bit the Tortoise nose (all) Joomi jo
Solo: This is the story my people (all) Joo mi jo

(Repeat this three times)

The Tortoise lost his nose. There was no reconstruction surgery done, thus the Tortoise nose remained very short until today!

Exercise

Write three lessons this story has taught you.

139 Senufo mask called *kponiugo* representing a mythical being who protects the community from sorcerers and soul-stealers. He is represented with the jaws of a hyena, the tusks of a wart-hog, the horns of an antelope and of some other creature. Appropriately the mask is intended to recall the chaos before the world was set in order. Between the horns are a hornbill and a chameleon, two of the primordial animals. The chameleon's slow and careful walk is due to the fact that he was the first creature to walk on the newly formed surface of the earth. These masks appear in groups after dark and appear to spit fire, for tinder is held in a cleft stick in front of the mouth. Courtesy of the Art Institute of Chicago. L. 40¼ in.

An example of Yoruba Poetry

ISE NI OOGUN ISE

ISẸ́ NI ÒÓÒGUN ÌSẸ́
JOB IS THE MAGIC MEDICINE FOR POVERTY

MÚRA SÍ ISẸ́ ÒRÉẸ̀ MI
KEEP WORKING HARD MY FRIEND

ISẸ́ LÀA FI ŃDENI GÍGA
HARD WORK WILL MAKE YOU GREAT

BÍ A KÒ BÁ RẸ́NI FẸ̀HÌN TÌ
IF YOU ARE NOT A DEPENDANT OF NO ONE

BÍ ÒLE LÀÁ RÍ
YOU FEEL LIKE A LAZY PERSON

BÍ AKÒ BÁ RẸ́NI GBẸ́KẸ̀LÉ
IF YOU HAVE NO ONE TO LEAN ON

À TẸRA MÓ SẸ́ ẸNI
YOU BETTER KEEP ON WORKING

BÀBÁ RE LEÈ LÓWÓ LỌ́WÓ
ALTHOUGH YOUR DADDY MAY BE RICH

ÌYÁ RE SI LEÈ L'ẸSIN LÉEKAN
AND MOM MAY HAVE HORSES IN THE

STABLE

BÍ O BÁ GBÓJÚ LÉ WON
IF YOU JUST DEPEND ON THEM

O TẸ́ TÁN NI MO SỌ FÚN Ẹ
YOU ARE OPENING A PANDORA DOOR TO

POVERTY

MÁ F' ÒWÚRÒ SERÉ ÒRÉẸ̀ MI
DON'T WASTE YOUR EARLY YEARS MY

FRIEND

MÁRA SÍ SẸ́ OJỌ́ ŃLỌ
WORK HARD, TIME IS RUNNING OUT

284

An Example of Yorùbá Myth

The Yorùbá myth is traditional stories often found on some facts of nature or an event in the early history of the Yorùbá people. They serve the purpose of giving meaning to existence and ensuring that the community does not lose hold of its rationale for existence. Some of these myths are embodying in religious beliefs, imaginary persons, things, or events.

An example of Yorùbá myth with significant philosophy is the "Kádàrá" or "Àyànmọ́" myth that is a belief in predistination. This seems to suggest that the Yoruba have the need to be less anxious about life. Thus, they believe that whatever happens to them in life, has been preordained by God. Therefore, they feel helpless to control situations that seem to be a validation of "Àyànmọ́ or Kádàrá."

Yoruba Fables

Other Yorùbá moral sciences include fables which involve elements of supernatural. The story of Òro ìrókò (Ìrókò Tree Deman), the son of a farmer was trapped on a tree that was being cut down by a demon. The boy had three magic gourds in his pocket. Each time the demon was about to succeed in cutting the tree, the boy would throw one gourd and the tree would be joined together again. When the boy was left with the last magic gourd, he felt he was at risk of being killed. Fortunately, he remembered the flute and the song his father taught him for such a time as this. He then sang it, hence the demon felt good and slept off; the son was able to escape.

There are numerous particles in Yoruba language, these particles may be in unit form, however, they bind the big stands of syllables together to form a meaningful concept. Some of them are used for grammatical purposes as well as for agglutination. However, their vowels are omitted without damaging the general meaning of the concept. These particles are omitted in written words and in conversation, in order to avoid ambiguities. The root vowels are 'a' 'e' 'ẹ' 'i' 'o' 'ọ'u

YORÙBÁ, ÈPÀ HEADDRESS #14, 12", Nigeria $275

The works from the Èpà association honor deities and cultural heroes at masked festivals. The large base heads, of deceased ancestors, are treated with less naturalism than the superstructure, which depicts and honors mothers with children, warrior/hunters, animals and rulers with their entourages in impressive sculptural form.

A-bà-village

A-bẹ - Knife, ma fi Abe sere, ma <u>fabe</u> sere = don't play with knife

A-bí - to born

A-bọ - to worship an idol

A-bo - female

A-bú - to insult

À-dá - a cutlass

A-dì - to pack up

A-dó - name of a city in Oyo state

A-dú - to kill an animal

A-fẹ́ - we want

A-fọ̀ - we washed, a fo aso, a foso

À-ga - a chair, o gaga, instead of ogun aga

Bà (<u>bà</u>-ọ́jẹ́)	To ruin somebody's reputation
Ba (<u>ba</u> - irun)	To braid one's hair
Ba (<u>bá</u> - á lé)	The most elderly in a community or village chief
Bẹ (<u>be</u>-jù)	too forward
Bẹ́ (<u>Bé</u>-lulè)	To fall off
Bẹ́ẹ̀ (<u>bẹ́ẹ̀</u>-bẹ́ẹ̀)	so on and so forth or it is far
Bẹ́ẹ̀ (<u>bệ</u>-kọ́)	not so (or) no
Bẹ́ẹ̀ (<u>bệ</u>-ni)	Yes, or that's right

Bí (bí-mo)	to deliver a new baby or to bear a new child
Bi (bí-mo)	If I or (bi-o) if he/she
Bi (bi-léerè)	to ask him or her a question
Bí (bí-I-tìre' or bíi-tì'rẹ)	like yours
Bí (bi-kò bá sì'rẹ)	If not you
Bì (bì)	To throw up (vomit)
Bó (bo')	To peel off
Bo (bọ́-síle)	Fell on the ground
Bọ́ (bọ́-ọmọ)	To feed the baby
Bọ'o	Feeding somebody or something
Bọ́ (bọ́-ojú)	To wash one's face
Bọ (bọ-òrisà)	To worship orisa (god)
Bú (bú-u)	To verbally abuse someone
Dà (dà-gba)	To become older
Dá (dá owó)	To donate money
Da (da'lẹ̀)	To betray someone
Dà (òun dà?)	(Locative) where is (it, she, he)
Dé (Mo-dé)	I arrive
Dé (Mo-dé-fìlà)	I wear a cap
Dè (mo-dè)	To tie something up
Dí (ona-ti-di)	The road is blocked
Di (Di-ọla)	Till tomorrow
Di (Di-irun)	To roll one's hair

288

Ẹ̀ (Ẹ̀-yin)	Word for ìwo=you
Ẹ (ẹ-gbà)	You take (In plural)
Fǎ (fǎ-gùn)	To prolong
Fàá (fàǹtẹ́ẹ̀ tẹ́)	Teaching a child how to walk
Fá (fá-irungàbọ̀n)	To shave one's head
Fà (Tóny fà ju)	Tony is too sluggish
Fẹ́ (mo-fẹ́-èyí)	I like this
Fẹ (mo-fẹ́-ni-iyàwó-kan)	I want a wife
Fẹ̀ (máse-fẹ̀)	Do not brag
Fi (kí-lo-fi-se)	What did you use it for
Fi (ta lo fi hàn)	Who showed it/him or her
Fi (Kílo fi fún)	What did you give him/her
Fi (Kí-lo-fi-pò)	What did you mix it with
Fi (kí-lo-fi-rán)	What did he/she send
Fi (Fi-sí-bẹ̀)	To put it there
Fi (fi-àkókò-sòfò)	To waste time
Fi (fi-pamọ́)	To keep something
Fi (fi-owo-pamọ)	To keep the money
Fi (fi-ara-pamo)	To hide oneself
Fí (fí-orúkọ-sílè)	To register, enlist
Fi (Fi-ife-mu omi)	To drink water with a cup
Fi (Fi-ọgbọ́n-àgbà-gbe)	Crystallized intelligence
Fi (fi-sílẹ)	Leave him/her or it alone

Fi (fi-owó-si)	Endorse it
Fi (fi-si-nú)	To put inside (like grudge)
Fi (Igi-nâ-nfi)	To shake
Fò	To jump, (fo-okùn) - to jump rope
Fó	To break (Awò-nâ-fó), the plate broke
Fò	To wash one's teeth, (Mo-fọ ehín-mì)
Fọn	To blow, (fon-fèrè), to blow a whistle
Fún	To give, (fun mi ní omi) give me some water
Fún	To give (fun mi no owó) give me some money
Ga	To be tall, (Ilé na ga) the house is tall
Gé	To cut, cut my hand with a knife, (mo fi-ọbè gé aràmi lówọ́)
Gé	To bite, (gé je, mo géejẹ), I bite him/her or it
Gbà	To receive or take, (gba gbogbo ògo) - take all the glory.
Gbá	To sweep, (gba'lè) to sweep the floor.
Gba	To take, (gbà ibí) take this way.
Gbà	To allow, (gbâ làayé) to give him/her a chance
Gba	Ìmọ̀nràn, to take advice
Gbé	To get married (gbe'yawo) get married
Gbé	To live (níbo lòn gbé) where do you live?
Gbe	To carry to life, (gbé ga) to be elevated
Gbe	To steal, (kini ole gbe) - what did the thief steal

Gbẹ́	To dig up (Tuńdé ti gbe ilẹ na) Tuńdé had dug the ground
Gbẹ	To dry up (asọ na ti gbẹ) the cloth is dry.
Gbìn	To plant, (mo gbin àgbàdo) I planted maize
Gbó	To bark, (ajá ńgbó) the dog is barking
Gbo-gbo	All (gbogbo wà nıyí) here is all of us
Gbọ	To hear, (mo gbóẹ) I hear you
Há	To be tight, (ha wọ́) to be tight fisted
Ha	To scare, (mo ha mó mi) don't scare me
Hó	To boil, (omí ti hó) the water is boiling
Hó	To make noise, (nwọń hó lhó ayò) they made a joyful noise
Họ	To run, (Bóla ho fuń ajṇ) Bola ran from a dog
Họ	To scratch (Túndeď bámi ho ẹhìn mi) please Tunde scratch my back for me)
Hù	Germinate (isu na ti hù) the yam germinates
Hú	To uproot, (Wálé ti hú ata na) Walé uprooted the paper tree
Jà	To fight (Bímpé àti Bóla jà) Bímpé and Bóla fought
Já	To break as in (gẹ́ mo já okùn ńa) I broke the rope
Jẹ	To eat, (mo fẹ́ jẹ èwà) I want to eat beans
Jẹ	To eat food, (mo ti jẹun) I have eaten
Jí	To wake up, (Mo tètè ji) I woke up early

Ji´	To steal, (olè ji´mi lówó) the thief stole my money
Jó	To dance, (mó fẹ́ jó) I want to dance
Jó	To get burnt, (Ilé ńjó) the house is burning
Jò	To leak out, (ife na ńjò) the cup is leaking
Jọ	To look alike, that boy looks like me (ọmọ kùnrín na jọ mí)
Jọ̀	To filter, (mo jǒ kúnná) I filtered it smoothly
Ka	To read, (ka ìwé) read the book
Ka	To count, (ka owó) count the money
Ké´	To shout (ké-igbe) to shout loudly
Ke	To cut (ke simeji) cut into two
Kẹ´	To pet, (ké-mi) pet me
Ki´	To greet, (Mo Kíi) I greet him/her
Ko´	To move out (kó kúrò) move away
Ko	To collect, (Kó ilè) to collect or park the trash
Kòó	To meet (lójà ni mo ti kò ó) I met him at the market
Kọ́	To build, (kó-ilé) to build a house
Ko	To teach, (kó ní èkó) teach him/her lesson
Kọ	To write, (ko léta) write a letter
Kọ	To be first, (èmi ló kó parí) I finished first
Kọ̀	To refuse, (Kò jálè) refuse vehemently.
Kọ́	To study (Kọ́-èkó)
Kú´	To die, (bàbá wa àgàba ti kú) our grand papa has died

Kù	To remain, (ó kù díè̩)
Kù	The sound of thunder, (ò̩jò̩ n̄kù)
La	To leak, (aja ńla awó rè̩) the dog licks his plate
La̩a	To survive something, (Mo la̩ ja) I survived it
Là	To be affluent (ìdílé wa là) our family is affluent
Le	To be tough or difficult (ìsirò̩ nâ le) the math problem is difficult
Le	can or able (mo le s̩é) I can do it
Le̩	to be lazy, (o̩mo̩ nâ le̩) the boy is lazy
Lo	to use (mo lo síbí) I use the spoon
Lo̩	to go, (mo lo̩ sí ilé̩ we) I want to go to school
Lo̩	to grind, (mo lo̩ ata) I grinded the pepper
Lo̩	to iron, (Mo lo as̩o mi) I ironed my cloth
Lu	to beat, (Túndé ló lu o̩mo̩ nâ) Túndé beat up the boy
Lù	to beat a drum, (Bádé mo̩ ìluú lù) Bádé knows how to drum very well
Má	do not, (mâ bínú símí) don't be up set with me
Má	do not, (mâ do ju timi) don't let me down
Mà	to recognize, (ma mà yín) I know you
Mi	mine, (tè mí nìyi) this is mine
Mì	to swallow, (mo gbé omi mì) I swallowed the water
Mí	to be breathing, (ejò̩ nâ ńmí') the snake is breathing
Mì	be shaking (sá má mì bí okò̩ le jò) just keep shaking,

293

	even if you can't dance
Mo	I, me (mo ti se tán) I have finished
Mọ́	no more, (kò sí mọ́) there is no more
Mọ́	Clean, aso na mo (the cloth is clean)
Mọ	to construct or to build, mo mo'ikòkò amọ̀ built a pot with mud
Mú	to take, (mo mú òbe dání) I am holding a knife
Mu	to drink (mo mu omi) I, drank water
Mù	to be so hidden (ona ile'Dele mù) the way to Dele's house is hidden
Ná	to spend money, (Màmá ná owó mi) Mama spent my money
Ná	to bargain/to price goods/hazzle (mo ná ẹran nâa wò) I priced the meat
Ni	to have, (mo ní) I have
Ni	to be the person in question, (òun ni) or emi ni eg) the question may be who threw the rock ans=èmini, òun ni, àwa ni, or àwon ni
Nu	to clean, (nǔ nùn) clean it up
O	You, (sé o gbọ́) did you hear me
O	She/he/it (ó gbọ́e) he/she or it hear you
Ọ	You, (mo fún o lówo) I gave you the money

Pa	to kill (Olá pa e ku) Ola killed the rat
Pa	to turn off the light (pa iná, 'Dayò) turn the light off 'Dayò, Day ọ pa iná
Pa	to ask about how much money someone has made, (Èló lo pa) how much money have you made
Pè	to call (ta ló pè mí) who called me
Pe´	that what, (pe kini)
Pé	to be late, (kí lo ṣe pé bẹ̀) why did you come so late
Pé	to dodge something/or somebody, (mo pé aja na si lẹ) I dodge the dog
Pe´	that what, (pe kini)
Pe	to be late, (kí lo ṣe pe be) why did you come so late
Pé	to dodge something/or somebody, (mo pé ajá nâ sí lẹ) I dodge the dog
Rà	To buy (babá ra bàtà fún mi) daddy bought me a show
Rá	to have lost (owó tí Túndé fi ta tétẹ rá) 'Túndé lost money in gambling
Re	To harvest pepper, (Ade nre ata) Ade harvesting paper
Rẹ	yours (ti re) it is yours
Rè	his/her/its (ti rè) it is his or her's or its
Rẹ	to soak something (Délé rẹ aṣọ nâ sínú ose) 'Dele soak the cloth in the soap
Ré	to cut (mo re je) I cut you short/I cheat you.

Re	to cut off (mo re kúrò) I cut off
Ri	to see, (Mo rí ran) I can see
Ri	to immerse/soak (ọde rí aṣọ na si nu omi) Adé immersed or soak the cloth in the water
Ro	to be in pain (ehin ńro Túndé) Túndé is feling pain in his back
Ro	difficult (ọdún kò ni ro fún wa) the year will not be difficult for us
Ro	leaks/drops of liquid (omi ńro láti àjà) water is dropping from the ceiling
Ro	to weed off, (bàbá ro oko rẹ̀) daddy weeded his farm
Ro	to stir up, (mo ro ọbẹ̀ na pọ̀) I stirred up the soup.
Ro	to wrap a wrapper, (ọkùnrin kìí ró ìró) men don't wrap a wrapper
Rò	to think (mo rò pe ọ̀jò fẹ́ rò) I think it is going to rain.
Ro	to be paralyzed, (ẹsẹ̀ ọmọ na rọ) the child's leg is paralyzed.
Rọ̀	to soften up, (isu na rọ̀ ńigbati a see) the yam had softened up after it was boiled.
Rọ́	to have a broken bone, (omo nà fi ẹsẹ̀ rọ́) the boy broke his leg.
Rọ̀ọ́	to plea someone, (baba rọ Jide ki ko mase ja mo) Daddy pleaded to Jide to stop fighting.

Rù to have lost weight (Tìtí ti rù) Titi has lost a lot of weight.

Ru to carry a luggage on the head, (Yemí ru gbogbo ẹrù na) Yemí, caries all the luggage on his head

Sá to run, (Titílayò le sáré) Titílanyò can run

Sa to gather, (Ọlá sa ilẹ̀ jọ) Olá gathered the trash together

Se to cook, (mo fẹ́ràn láti se ọbẹ̀) I like to cook soup

Se to request to be left alone (se fún mi) just leave me alone

Si (Preposition) to/on, (mo fi owó sí orí àga) I left the money on the chair.

Sọ to say (so fún mi) tell me

Sọ to throw away, (Mo sọ owó nù) I lost some money

Ṣé questioning/answer, (Ṣé tèmi nìyí) is this mine

Ṣe to do, (Mo ti se tán) I have finished

Se it's a pitty, (ó mà se ò)

Ṣẹ́ to deny (Judas: ṣẹ́ Jesu) Judas had denied Jesus.

Ṣẹ̀ to offend someone, (òrẹ́ mi ṣẹ̀ mi) my friend has offended me.

Sọ to yell, (Mo sọ fún) I told him/her

Sò to grumble (má sò mọ́) stop grumbling

Sòọ to watch, (Mò ń sọọ) I am watching him/her

Ta to sting, (Kòkòrò ta mí) the ant had stung me

Ta to shoot, (Bádé ta ìbon) Bádé shot the gun

Tán to finish, (mo ti se tan) I have finished

Tàn	to deceive, (má se tàn mí) don't deceive me
Tan	to relate with someone, (mo bá e tan) I am related to you
Tẹ	to be let down, (máse jékín tẹ) don't let me down
Tẹ́	to lay (mo tẹ́ ibùsùin mi) I layed my bed
Tẹ	to print, (ta ló tẹ ìwé na) who printed the book
Tẹ̀	to bow down (Ó tẹ̀ fún mi) he/she bow down for me
Tẹ̀	to press on (ó tẹ̀ mí mólè) he/she stepped on me
Ti	that of, (ti tani) whose is that
Tì	to close (Ilè kùn na ti) the door is locked
Tòó	to arrange, (Jòwó bá mi tòó) please help to arrange it
Tọ́	to raise, (èmi ló tó ọmọ nà dàgbà) I raised the child
Tọ̀	to urinate (mó fẹ tò) I want to urinate
Tọ̀	to take a route (ọnà wo lo tọ̀) which route did you take
Tu	to throw out, (ọmọ na tu ounjẹ rẹ) the baby threw out the food
Tú	to untie (mo tú okùn bàtà mi) I untie my shoes
Tùú	to pet/calm down, (ẹbá mi tùú) help me to calm him/her down
Wá	come (ẹ wá) come over
Wà	exit (Ọlọ́run wà) God exits
Wá	to seach, (kí lò ń wá? what are you searching for?
Wa	ours (ti wa ǹiyí) this is yours
Wà	(Location) to be in place, (nîbo ló wà?) Where have you been?
Wa	to drive a car, (mo wa okò mi) I drove my car

Wé	to wear a head scarf, (mọ́mọ̀ wé gèlè) mother wear a head scarf
Wé	To compare with, (mọ́ se fi ọmọ wé omo) don't compare a child with another child
Wẹ́	So little (Àwon ọsàn na wẹ́) the oranges are too small
Wẹ̀	to take a bathe,'(Dayọ̀ ti lo wẹ̀) Dayọ̀ has gone to take his bath
Wí	to say, (mo wí fuń ọ) I told you
Wì	to barbeque, (mo wi adìẹ na) I barbeque the chicken
Wo	to look at / watch (wá wo tèmi) come see mine
Wọ	to wear, (Dayọ̀ wọ aṣọ rẹ) Dayọ wear his shirt
Wọ	to take a bus (mo wọ boosi) I took a bus
Wọ́	to creep as a snake (ejò na ti wo lo) the snake had creeped away.
Won	to be expensive (okò na wọn) the car is expensive
Wù	to like, (ọmọ bìnrin na wù mí) I like the girl
Ya	To become (Bọ́sẹ̀ ti ya nkan míran)'Bọ́sẹ̀ has become something else
Yà	to draw (wo ohun ti moyà) see what I drew
Yá	to borrow (yá mi lóbẹ) let me borrow your knife
Yán	to yawn, (wo bi o ti yan) see how him/her yawn
Yẹ̀	unfilfill, (Ileri re ko gobodo yẹ) you must fulfill your promise
Yẹ	to fit (adé ye mí) the crown fits me
Yí	to roll (yi okuta kuro) roll the stone away
Yìι	this (e yi ni mo fe) I want this
Yìn	to praise (mo yìn ọ́) I praise you
Yín	to turn, (yín redio yín sílẹ̀ or yin redio) turn the radio down

Yó — to be full, (Mo yó) I have eaten enough food

Yọ́ — to stalk, (yó tẹ̀ le) stalks after him/her

Yọ — to subtract, (yọ eji kúrú nínu ẹta) 3-2=

Yọ — to remove, (màmá yọ ẹgún lẹ́sẹ̀ mi) Mother removed the thorn from

my toe

Yọ̀ — to rejoice, (mo bá ẹ yọ̀) I rejoice with you

APPENDIX I
Countries of Africa and Languages Spoken

COUNTRY	LANGUAGES	SCRIPT
Algeria, Al Djazair, Algerie, (Democratic and Popular Republic of)		Aribic, latin, Berber
Angola, (Republic of)		Latin Bantu
Benin former kingdom, situated in present-day SW Nigeria	French and Fon	Latin fon
Botswana, (Republic of)	English is the official language, but the population is mainly Tswana, who speak a Bantu language	Latin
Burkina Faso or Burkina formerly Upper Volta	French is th official language	Latin
Burundi, Republic of	official languages are french and Kurndi (a Bantu language, Swahili is also spoken	Latin, Bantu
Cameroon (Cameron) Republic of	French and English are the official languages	Latin
Central African Republic (Republique Centrafricaine)	French is the official language, but Sango is the medium of communication among people who speak different language	Latin

Chad, (Republic of)	French and Arabic are the official languages	Latin
Congo, Republic of	French and Arabic are the official languages	Latin and others
Egypt (Arab Republic of Egypt)	Arabic is the official language	Arabic
Equatorial Guinea (Guinea Equatorial) Republic of	Spanish is the official language, but the majority speak a Bantu language	Latin
Ethiopia (republic)	The official language is Amharic, but English is widely spoken and the various ethnic groups speak their own languages	Latin Amharic
Gabon (Republique Gabonaise, or Gobonese Republic	English is the official language, but several Bantu dialects are spoken	Latin
The Gambia (Republic of)	English is the official language, but the Malinke language is common and wolof also is spoken	Latin

Ghana (Republic of)	English is the official language, but there are various linguistic groups, including the skan (Ashanti and Fanti), Mole-Dagbani, Ewe and GaAdangme, plus a number of indigenous dialects.	Latin and others
Guinea, Guinee (Republic of)	French is the main language, but a number of indigenous dialects are spoken	Latin
Ivory coast (Cote d'Ivoire)	French is the official language	Latin
Kenya (Republic of)	Swahili is the official language, but English is used in commerce	Latin
Lesotho (Kingdom of)	English and Sesotho, a Bantu Language are official languages, but Zulu and Ethosa are also spoken	Latin
Liberia (Republic of)	English is the official language, but tribal tongues are also spoken	Latin

Libya, (Socialist People's Libyan Arab Jamahirya)	Arabic is the official language	Arabic
Madagscar, (Democratic Republic	French and Malagsy are the official language	Latin
Malawi (Republic of	English and Chichewa are the official languages	Latin
Mali (Republic of)	French is the official language, but most of the population speaks Bambura	Latin
Mauritania Republique Isamike du Mauritanie(Islamic Republic of)	Arabic and wolof are the official languages French is also spoken	Aric, Latin
Morocco (Kingdom of)	Official language is Arabic, also spoken are Berber dialects, French (a main language of commerce) and Spanish	Arabic, Latin
Mozambique (Republic of)	Portuguese is the official language, but Afrikaans is widely spoken	Latin
Namibia, (Republic of)	English is the official language, but Haua and Djerma are widely spoken	Latin

Niger (Republic of)	English is the Official language, but Hausa and Djerma are widely spoken	Latin
Nigeria, (Federal Republic of)	English is the official language, but Hausa, Yoruba, Ibo and number of indigenous languages are regionally important.	Latin
Rwanda, (Republic of)	Kinyarwanda, and French are the official languages, but Swahilili also predominates	Latin
Senegeal, (Republic of Senegal)	French is the official language	Latin
Sieraa Leone (Republic of)	English is the original language, but Krio, a mixture of English and regional dialects is the lingua franca.	Latin
Somalia	Somalia is the official language, but Arabic English, and Italian are also spoken	Latin, Arabic

South Africa (Republic of)	English, Afrikaans, Sotho, Xhosa, Zulu, and six other African languages	Latin
Sudan (Republic of the Sudan)	Arabic is the official language and the predominant language in the North. Nilotic languages are spoken in the West and South. English is also spoken	Latin
Swaziland Windom of)	English and Siswati are the official languages	Latin
Tanzania (United Republic of)	Swahili and English are the official languages	Latin
Togo, (Republique Togolaise)	French is the official language. The ewe in the south and Voltaic-speaking peoples in the north are the main ethnic groups	Latin
Tunisia (Tunisie, Repulic of)	Arabic is the official language, but French also predominates	Latin

Uganda, (Republic of)	English is the official language, Swahili, Nilotic and Bantu languages are **widely spoken.**	Latin
Zaire, (Republic of) Formerly Republic of Congo	French is the official language, but Swahili and Lingala are widely spoken	Latin
Zambia, (Republic of) formerly Northern Rhodesia	English is the official language, but 98% of the inhabitants speak Bantu languages. Tonga, Nyanja and Bemba are some of those other languages	Latin
Zimbabwe (Republic of) Zimbabwe means "stone houses" in Bantu language	English is the official language, but the Shona and Ndebele speak in their native languages	Latin

APPENDIX II

SOCIAL FACTS IN NIGERIA

1. Men average life expectancy at birth is 54 years, as compared with 76 years inthe US
2. (Only 56% of the people live in urban area, as compared with about 76% in the US
3. Nigeria has the highest population in Africa about 140 million
4. Nigeria's external debts are the highest in Africa
5. (Conflict exists between notherners, who are mainly Muslim, and southerners who are Christians or followers of African religions
6. Nigeria's great artistic and historical centers include Nok, Ife (Oyo and Benin)

KEYPOINTS IN RECENT HISTORY

1914	Britian forms the colony of Nigeria
1960	Nigeria became an independent federation October 1
1966	Military leaders overthrew the civilian government
1967	Civil war broke out and the Eastern state of Biafra proclaims its independence
1970	Civil war ends with Biafra's defeat
1979	Civilian-rule is restored
1983	A military regime is established
1993	Presidential elections were annulled and military rule under General Sani Abacha continued
1995	The commonwealth suspended Nigeria's membership
1998	Abacha died and his successors continued the process of restoring civilian government
1999	Obansanjo Olesegun was elected president as Nigeria returned to civilian rule.

Information About the Republic of Nigeria

Location:	West Africa, on the Gulf of Guinea
Neighbors:	Benin, Niger, Chad, Cameroon
Official Name:	Federal Republic of Nigeria
Divisions:	Thirty states and the Federal Capital Territory
Capital	Abuja
Largest Cities:	Lagos, Ibadan, Kano, Ogbomosho
flag:	The Nigerian flag has three broad vertical stripes of equal width. The two outer stripes are of green, which represent agriculture. The stripe in the center is white, which stands for unity and peace.
National Anthem:	"Arise Ol compatriots, Nigeria's call obey"
Major Languages:	English(official), Hausa, Yoruba, lbo, Fulani
Currency:	Naira and Kobo

GEOGRAPHY

With an area of 356,669 square miles (923,769 sq.1km) Nigeria is Africa's fourteenth largest country. It is about 1.33 times bigger than Texas in the United States. (US).

Northern Nigeria consists of high plains and plateus, which are drained by the Niger and Benue Rivers. But in the northeast rivers, drain into Lake Chad, which occupies an inland drainage basin. Lake Chad, shares with Niger Republic, Cameroon Republic, the largest lake.

Southern Nigeria contains hilly regions and broad plains. The land rises to the southeast, with highlands among the border with Cameroon. Nigeria's highest point, Vogel Peak, reaches 6,669 ft (3,033m) in these highlands. Nigeria's coastline, contains many lagoons and the huge Niger delta is 478 miles (769 km) long.

Nigeria has tropical climate. The south is hot and wet, because there is rainfall throughout the year. Covered by dense rain forests, however, large areas have been cleared for farming. The north is hotter and drier. Dry season starts from November until March. Tropical Savannah merges into thorn scrubs in the far north.

ECONOMY

Chief farm products: Beans, beef, hides and skins cocoa, cassava, corn, cotton, millet, palm products, peanuts, rice rubber yams

Chief mineral resources: Oil and natural gas

Chief Industrial Products: Cement, chemicals, fertilizers, food Products, textiles, vehicles

Chief Export-   Oil (98%)

Per Capital Income: $280 (as compared with $29,089 in the United States. In the US, agriculture employs 3% of the work force, industry 26% and services 71%)

YORUBA TIMELINE

600S on Emergence of Ife Kingdom	1862 Ibadan Empire established in Nigeria and becomes most powerful in the region	1967-1970 Biafran (Nigerian Civil) War between Yoruba and northern Nigerians against easterners (mainly Igbo) secessionists	1993 In Nigeria transition from military rule to democratic rule ends when general Sanni Abacha declares himself ruler

1300s Bronze and terra-cotta sculpture produced in Ife, Oyo state founded	1897 British conquest of Yorubaland completed	1970s-1980s Series of failed civilian governments and military groups in Nigeria	1999 Nigeria returns to civilian rule with Olsegan Obasanjo, a Yoruba as President. He won another four-year term in 2003
1510 Start of Atlantic Slave trade	1950s Discovery of petroleum deposits in Nigeria	1974 Oil boom in Nigeria	
1789 Oyo Empire reaches greatest extent	1960 Nigeria wins independence	1975 Capital of Nigeria transferred from Lagos to Abuja	
1836 Oyo, dominated by Sokoto Caliphante: Oyo dissolves			

Comparative Language

YORUBA	ENGLISH	FRENCH	SPANISH
KAABQ	WELCOME	BIEN VENU A LA MAISON	VIENBENIDOS
OMINIRA	FREEDOM	LIBRE LIBERTE'	LIBERTAD
OSEUN	THANK YOU	MERCI	GRACIAS
ECO NI	HOW MUCH	COMBIEN	CUANTO
ODAABO	BYE BYE	NURE VIOR	ADIOS
KIN LORUKO RE	WHAT IS YOUR NAME?	COMMENT T 'APPELE	CUAL ES TU' NOMBRE
EKAARO	GOOD MORNING	BONJOUR	BUENOS DIAS
EKAA SAN	GOOD AFTERNOON	BONNE ARRE MIDI	BUENAS TARDES
EKA ALE	GOOD EVENING	BONSOR	BUENAS NOCHES
OMO ODUN MELO NI NIYIN?	HOW OLD ARE YOU?	QU 'ELLE VOUS? VOUS AVEZ QUEL AGE	CUAL ES TU HEDAD?
ALAFIA	PEACE	LA PAIX	PAZ
AWA FE ALAFIA	WE WANT PEACE	NOUS VOULONS LA PAIX	QUEREMOS PAZ
KO SI OGUN MO	NO MORE WAR NE PUS PAS LA GUERE	NE PUS PAS LAGUERE	NO MAS GUERRA
MO FERAN RE	I LOVE YOU	JE TAIME	YO TE QUIERO
MO FE JEOUN	I WANT TO EAT	JE VAIS MANQE	YO TE QUIERO
JE KAA LO	LET'S GO	VA T'ON	VAMONOS
BAWO NI?	HOW ARE YOU?	COMMENT VOUS	COMO ESTAS?
IFE NI IDAHUN	LOVE IS THE ANSWER	L 'AMOUR LA ES REPONSE	AMAR ES LA RESPUESTA
OFE	FREE	GRAJUIT	LIBRE
MO FERAN AMERICA	I LOVE AMERICA	J'AIME L'AMERIQUE	YO AMO A AMERICA

YORUBA	ENLISH	FRENCH	SPANISH
JOWO MA BINU	I AM SORRY	JE SUIS DESOLE	YO LO SIENTO
ALABUKUN NI MI	I AM BLESSED	JE SUIS BENTT	YO ESTOY BENDESIDO
IBUKUN NI FUN E	BLESS YOU	VOUS PROTEGE	BENDITO SEAS
DE'RIN	SLOW DOWN	DOU CE MENT	DESPASIO
YARA KIA	HURRY UP	RAPIDEMENT	RAPIDO
EKU ORII RE	CONGRATULATIONS	FELICITATION	FELICIDADES
MU OKAN	TAKE ONE	PREND UN	ILLEVATE UNO
MOTORO GAFARA	ESQUES ME	PARDONER MOI	DISCULPAME
FUN MI LO KAN	GIVE ME ONE	DONNE MOI	DAME UNO
NIBO LO NLO	WHERE ARE YOU GOING?	OU VOUS ALLER?	DONDE VAS?
IYEN DARA	THAT IS BEAUTIFUL	VOUS ETES TRES BELLE	ESO ES BERMOSO
MO FE ORILEDE YI	I LOVE THIS COUNTRY	J'AIME CETTE PAYE	YO AMO ESTE PAIS
NIBO NI OJA WA	WHERE IS THE MARKET?	OU EST LE MARCHE	DONDE ESTA EL MER CADO?
KIN NI AGOGO WI?	WHAT TIME IS IT?	IL EST QUEL HEURE	QUE HORA ES?
JOWO	PLEASE	SIL VOUS PLATT	POR FAVOR
JOWO NIBO NI OJA WA?	PLEASE WHERE IS THE MARKET PLACE?	SIL VOUS PLAIS OU SA SETROU VE LEMARCHE?	POR FAVOR DONDE ESTA EL MERCADO?
JE KI AJO SERE	LET'S PLAY TOGETHER	ON JOUE ENSEMBLE	VAMOS A JUGAR JUNTOS
MO FERAN RE TO BEE GE	I LOVE YOU VERY MUCH	JE T'AIME BE COUPS	YO TE GUIERO MUC HO

SINCE NEOLITHIC TIMES

since neolithic times.

Northern Africa

EASTERN AFRICA

Eastern Africa is Eritrea, Ethiopia, Djibouti, Somalia, Kenya, Uganda, Rwanda, Burundi, Tanzania, The Comoros Islands and Madagascar. The Indian Ocean and Red Sea are its coasts. The Great Rift Valley, some of the world's largest lakes, Africa's high and low points, forests, savannah and deserts are there. Madagascar's life forms are ancient and unique. Though it is entirely tropical, the highest elevations still get snow.

Eastern Africa's developing economies, some among the poorest in the world, rely on herding and agriculture. Recent wars further retard improvement. Scientists place man's earliest origin here. Ethiopia is 3,000 years old, Eritrea less than ten years old. Seafaring Arabs, then Europeans, dominated the Indian Ocean coast politically. Most of the area was under British rule before the 20th century brought independence.

Eastern Africa

WESTERN AFRICA

Western Africa is Benin, Burkina Faso, Cameroon, the Central African Republic, Gambia, Ghana, Guinea, Guinea-Bissau, the Ivory Coast, Liberia, Nigeria, Senegal, Sierra Leone and Togo. The southern coast and hinterlands of Africa's great western bulge, it covers most of geographical (not the country) Sudan. It lies between the Atlantic Ocean, Sahara Desert and Central African rain forest. The climate is tropical.

The area's developing economies rely heavily on agriculture and extractive industry. Overpopulation and drought are problems. The area was the home of such advanced native cultures as the 15th century Hausa. Most African slaves in the new world originated here. European control began in the 18th century and by the 20th only Liberia was self-governing. The area enters the 21st century completely independent.

Western Africa

SOUTHERN AFRICA

Southern Africa is Equatorial Guinea, Gabon, Congo, Zaire, Angola, Zambia, Malawi, Mozambique, Zimbabwe, Swaziland, the Republic of South Africa, Lesotho, Botswana, Namibia and Sao Tome. Its northern boundary is highlands rising from the Sahara, its eastern edge is the Great Rift Valley and the Indian Ocean. To the south and west is the Atlantic Ocean. The climate ranges from tropical in the north to subtropical in the south.

Southern African economies are mainly extractive and undeveloped. The industrialized Republic of South Africa, with a moderate climate and heavy European investment, dominates the area. The southern savannah and desert were inhabited very early but equatorial jungles were unpopulated until more recent times. In the 19th century, an expanding Zulu kingdom fought colonizing Europeans. Now native governments have replaced colonialism.

Southern Africa

Africa

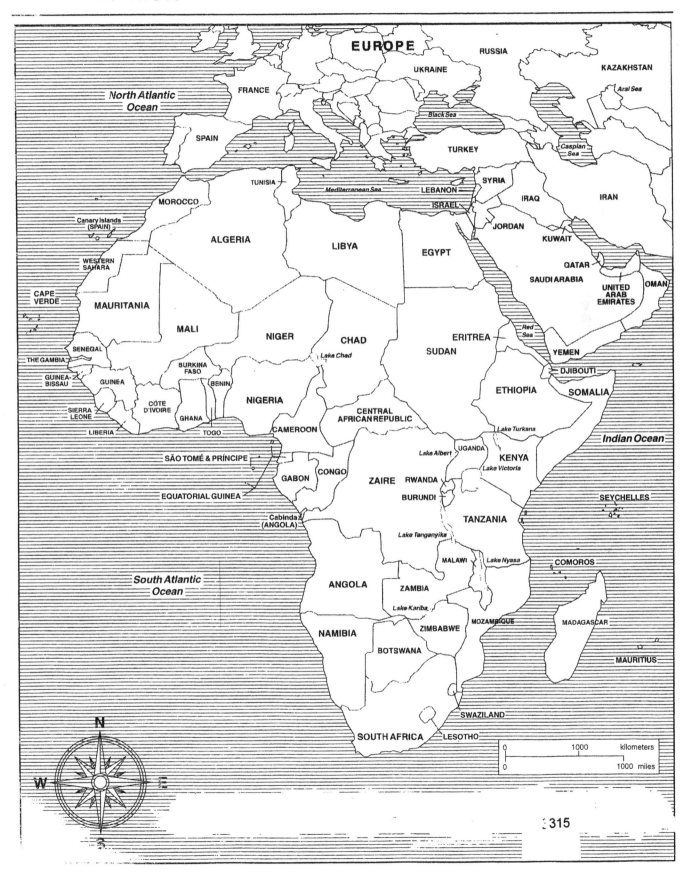

BIBLIOGRAPHY

Abraham, Roy Clive (1958) Dictionary of Modern Yoruba. London: University of London Press

Adebayo, G.A. (1975) Agbekaa Yoruba Yoruba Apa Keji: Ilesa Ilesanmi Press (language study: grammar)

Adeboyeje, A. (1985) Ede ati Girama Yoruba Lagos; Macmillan Nigeria

Adeoye, C. L. (1985) Igbagbo ati Esin Yoruba. Ibadam: Evans Brothers

Adesiuo V/A/ (1985) Ojulowo Girama Yoruba. Lagos: Pathway Publishers

Adetugbo, A. (1987) The Yoruba Language In Wester Nigeria: It's Major Dialect Areas. New York, Columbia University

Adeyemo, Bade. Yoruba as a Language of An Immediate Environment. Abeokuta, Nigeria Goad Publisher

Armstrong, Robert (1962) Yoruba Numerals. Oxford University Press

Ajayi, Bade (1998) Ojilelegbeta: Alo Apamo Yoruba, Illorun Tawfigullahi Publishing House

Ajibola, J. O. Owe Yoruba Ti a Tumo si ede, Oruko Yoruba fun ojo ose ati osu odin

Awosika, Soboyejo, In Pursuance of the Yoruba Legend, USA: Detta Congress, 1947

Bamgbose, A. (1966) A Grammar of Yoruba, Cambridge University

Bamgbose, Ayo (1967) A Short Yoruba Grammar, Iba Fau, London: Heinemann

Crowther, Samuel Ajayi (1870) A Vocabulary of the Yoruba Language (London: Church Missionary Society

Delano, Isaac O. A. (1965) Modern Yoruba Grammar, London: New York, T. Nelson

Delano, Isaac O. A. (1966) Owe l'e sin oro. Yoruba Proverbs: Their Meaning and Usage. Ibadan: Oxford University Press

A Dictionary of the Yoruba Language (1950) London: Oxford Press

Education: How Yoruba People Perform Academically, (May 2001 – January 2003) http://www.utexas.edu coc/Journalism/Source/J331/Yoruba.html

Fabunmi, M. A. (1969) Yoruba Idioms, Wande Abimbola, ed. (Lagos): Pilgrim Brooks.

Facts of File, Inc. (1997) Peoples of West Africa the Pilgrim's Group

Fafunwa, A.B., Bans. A History of Education in Nigeria. London: George Allen and Inwin, 1974, p. 99

Lucas, T. O. (1964) Yoruba Language, HS Structure and Relationship to Other Languages, Selly Oak Colleges, Birmingham, England

"National Association of Yoruba Descendants in North America," Tenth Yoruba National Convention. (May 21–June 2, 2003. January 27, 2003). http:www.Yorbanation.org. Education.html

Onayemu, A. O. (1999). Yoruba "Mooko, Mooke. Bis Bus International

Schieicher, A. F. (1993) Jeka so Yoruba, New Haven: Yale University Press

"Western Region Debates," History of Education in Nigeria (June 1952. January 27, 2003) http://usembassy.state gove/nigeia/www.hesc2.html

ISBN 141208531-4

9 781412 085311

Edwards Brothers Malloy
Oxnard, CA USA
April 7, 2015